# REFLECTIONS

## ON TALKS WITH SRI RAMANA MAHARSHI

*by* S.S. COHEN

BOOKS AVAILABLE BY THE SAME AUTHOR:
*Guru Ramana, Srimad Bhagavata, Forty Verses* and
*Advaitic Sadhana*

Sri Ramanasramam
Tiruvannamalai
INDIA

**REFLECTIONS ON TALKS WITH SRI RAMANA MAHARSHI** (English):
By S.S. Cohen

© Sri Ramanasramam, Tiruvannamalai

| | | |
|---|---|---|
| *First Edition* | : | *1959* |
| *Second Edition* | : | *1971* |
| *Third Edition* | : | *1979* |
| *Fourth Edition* | : | *1990* |
| *Fifth Edition* | : | *2006* |
| *Sixth Edition* | : | *2009* — *1000 copies* |
| Seventh Edition | : | 2013 |
| 1000 copies | | |

CC No. 1038
**ISBN: 978-81-88018-38-3**

Price: ₹ 90

*Published by*
**V.S. Ramanan**
President
Sri Ramanasramam
Tiruvannamalai 606 603
Tamil Nadu, INDIA

| | | |
|---|---|---|
| *Email* | : | *ashram@sriramanamaharshi.org* |
| *Website* | : | *www.sriramanamaharshi.org* |

*Typeset at*
Sri Ramanasramam, Tiruvannamalai

*Printed by*
Gnanodaya Press
Chennai 600 035
Tamil Nadu, INDIA

# PREFACE

To write a commentary on Sri Ramana Bhagavan's words, which are deemed to be lucidity itself, may seem to be a superfluous labour; yet there are thousands of studious seekers who have not had the privilege of hearing the teaching direct from the Master's lips, who would feel benefited and, indeed, happy to receive an exposition of it from those who have. For the sake of these I have culled from the compendious work, now the well-reputed *Talks with Sri Ramana Maharshi*, such gems and in such numbers as in my humble opinion can fairly and comprehensively represent the teaching, adding my own reflections, as "Notes", to each quotation which I have named "Text", to indicate its origin. I have, moreover, sifted and classified them in separate chapters so as to facilitate the study of each individual subject.

I deem it essential to give here a brief biography of the book in question. It is named "Talks" from being a record in the form of a diary of some of the conversations which the visitors and disciples have had with the Master on Spiritual matters for almost exactly four years — April 1935 to May 1939. In those years it used to be called "The Journal". For roughly half of this period it was written in the *Darshan* Hall itself by the diarist, or recorder, Sri M. Venkataramiah, the late Swami Ramananda Saraswati, at the end of each particular conversation at which he was present. Sri Bhagavan scarcely ever answered in English, but invariably in Tamil, which very often the diarist himself translated into English to the questioner within the hearing of the whole audience. But questions in Telugu and Malayalam,

Bhagavan answered in the same languages, and the answers in the latter language may be said to have been lost to the diarist, who did not understand Malayalam.

Therefore the language of this diary is of the recorder, more often it is a paraphrase of the Master's answers, occasionally His very words, rendered into English, for it was impossible to write down afterwards all He had said, or to keep pace with Him even if the answers were to be taken down verbatim on the spot. What we want is the Truth as expounded by Bhagavan, and this Truth is all here, which is all that matters.

As for the teaching of Sri Bhagavan, it has by now acquired a worldwide recognition, and has attracted earnest seekers from all the five Continents, as much for its fresh simplicity as for its sturdy rationality, which appeal both to the head and the heart. It can, however, be summed up in the ancient dictum "Know thyself", or "Seek the seeker", which the Master dins in one form or another in practically every answer he gives. Find out the questioner, he insists, and you will know the truth, which will solve all your problems and remove all your doubts.

Peace, by whatever name and in whatever guise it goes — happiness, knowledge, liberation, truth, etc. — is the conscious and unconscious aim and object of all human endeavour; for, the Master tells us, it is the very nature of our being, our very Self, so that self-seeking in the last analysis turns out to be a quest for Peace, from which there is no escape. There is no feeling, no thought, no action which does not stand on the foundation of Self. Self-preservation, or self-love is the dominant instinct in all life. When the Lord God commanded the Children of Israel in the wilderness to love their neighbour as themselves (Leviticus, XIX, 18), He meant that the maximum good that one man can do to another is to love him as much as he loves himself, self-love being the strongest of all passions, and the substratum of all emotions. We have no doubt heard of the self-immolation of many a mother for her child in cases of extreme danger, and of a patriot for his country, but the gratification derived from this immolation is to the Self. *My* child, *my* country, clearly denote the 'I', or Self, and what is immolated is only the body, and not the Self, which, being pure knowledge, pure spirit, can never be destroyed to be immolated.

We, therefore, seek the Self in everything, in every circumstance, and at every moment. It is self-love or self-seeking that induces us to desire, to work, to learn, to compete, to exert, to become politicians, administrators, scientists, black marketeers, gamblers, philanthropists, patriots, and finally yogis. It is self-love that makes us scour the skies, dig the earth and plumb the oceans. But alas, this self-seeking, being unintelligent, is sought outside the Self and thus succeeds only precariously, if at all. To seek the Self we have to go to the Self, not to the not-Self.

When people, therefore, group round the Master with bundles of problems, bundles of questions and grievances, he knows that they are seeking only the Self, and to the Self he turns them. "You are asking all these questions in the interest of your own self," he virtually tells them, "all your efforts have so far been directed for the good of this self of yours; now try to find out whether this good has been a genuine good, and this self is your true Self. You have been seeking this good in the wrong direction, in wrong things and wrong places, because you have been mistaken about your own identity. What you have been taking for yourself is not yourself at all. Your instinct of self-love has got mixed up with your sense-perceptions and brought you down to this strait. You fell victim to a hoax, from which to be saved you have taken the trouble to come to this Ashram with your load of worries and misery for luggage.

"Now what you should do is to learn what the Self is, and then directly seek it. Do not digress in irrelevant matters, in bodies, *koshas*, involution and evolution, birth and death, in supersensuous sights and sounds, etc., for all these are glamorous irrelevancies which trap and seduce you away from the reality of yourself and retain you in the delusion of the senses from which you are now attempting to escape. What is of importance is not what you perceive, think or do, but WHAT YOU ARE." Sense-perceptions, conceptions, sensations, actions, are mere dreams, mere pictures in the consciousness that perceives them. They rise from it, like dreams from the dreamer, distract its attention for a while and disappear in it. They change incessantly, have a beginning and an end, but he, the thinker and knower, being pure intelligence, remains ever. The knower is thus indestructible. The light of knowledge comes only from him, the subject, never from the object, the body. What we therefore call our Self is not the body, which is born, grows and dies, which is made of innumerable non-homogeneous parts which do not think, do not seek, do not perceive and do not understand. We are the intelligent indivisible unit 'I' — life itself — which pervades and uses the body, which sees but cannot be seen, hears but cannot be heard, smells but cannot be smelled, knows but cannot be known: for it is always a subject, never an object. And because we cannot see, hear or smell our 'I', we mistake it for the body which can be seen, heard and smelled. Thus the self-instinct, the 'I'-sense, getting mixed up with the sense perceptions, loses itself in the world of sense-percepts, from which none can save it but the Supreme Guide, the divine Guru.

Thus the knower, or dreamer, is alone real; the known is sheer dream. This sums up the teachings of the *Srutis*, and conforms to the experience of Sri Ramana Bhagavan.

To follow up the Quest till the Self is realised, is the path of *Jnana*, of Supreme Knowledge, of Liberation and Bliss everlasting — a path which has been viewed by the Master from every side and discussed in every detail. He has said everything that needs be said and revealed everything that needs be revealed. And whatever he has not said and revealed is scarcely worth knowing.

This is, therefore, the spiritual Kamadhenu,* which can satisfy the hunger of all Truth-seekers. The *sadhaka*, or yogi, who puts the teaching to the test will find in it ample material to guide him in his inner quest. What helps one *sadhaka* in his forward march may not help another; but every *sadhaka* will find in it the hints which will help him most to work out for himself the method of practice which suits him best and which is likely to lead him straight to the Goal. He who looks in it for long, detailed lectures on the rules of meditation and *samadhi*, as he is accustomed to do on the laws of physics and mathematics, will look in vain; for we do not deal here with sensuous problems and equations which can be verified and resolved in the common world of liquids and solids, of durations and dimensions, but with the obstacles of the seeking mind itself to perceive its own native state — obstacles which none can remove but the very same mind through self-investigation and self-control, without the help of any sensuous medium or scientific instrument.

**Vellore.** **S. S. C**

---

* The Celestial Cow which grants all boons, of edibles in particular.

# CONTENTS

# CHAPTER ONE

# HAPPINESS AND MISERY

1.  "How to avoid misery?" The Master answers: "Has misery a shape? Misery is only an unwanted thought. The mind is not strong enough to resist it. It can be strengthened by worship of God."                    241*

*Note*: Bhagavan at the very outset drives to the heart of the human problems, which are the consequences of man's delinquencies, thoughtlessness, desires, sins, etc., namely, misery. He tries to open men's eyes by asking, "Has misery a shape?" Surely misery is not a solid, heavy object which can descend on our heads and crush us. It is a purely mental phenomenon, a mere thought, which can be driven away with a little effort by a strong mind. But unfortunately the minds of men are generally weakened by lack of control, strong attachment, selfishness, and ignorance, so that they stand always at the mercy of every calamity that comes their way. Bhagavan suggests some methods of strengthening the mind. The worship of God is probably one of the easiest. The contemplation of the highest, purest, and most sublime ideal elevates the mind, and for the time being shuts out all other thoughts, including those that cause misery. By degrees the mind acquires purity and balance, and so, permanent peace, which no calamity can shake.

---

* The figure marked at the end of each quotation represents the number of the section in the *Talks* from which it has been taken.

2.   "I have no peace of mind. Something prevents it —
     probably my destiny." Bhagavan answers: "What is
     destiny? There is no destiny. Surrender and all will be
     well. Throw all the responsibility on God. Do not bear
     the burden yourself. What can destiny do to you then?"

                                                    244

*Note*: The questioner is a lady — a Maharani — in great
mental distress. Bhagavan is touched. He gives the solace
that everything is borne by God, and on Him all one's burden
should be laid through surrender. This appears to play a
tune different from the previous answer, where the worship
of God has been recommended. Here the tune is "surrender",
which amounts practically to the same thing as worship
through contemplation. Contemplation or meditation is also
surrender; for relinquishing all thoughts but that of the
meditation is relinquishing the whole world. In fact cessation
of thinking is the greatest of all surrender. Although
meditation can be sustained for only a limited time every
day, it becomes very powerful if repeated daily for years.

   By "there is no destiny" Bhagavan does not mean that
there is no *prarabdha:* we are all agreed that there is, but his
meaning is that once we surrender genuinely and truly,
*prarabdha* will pass us by unnoticed: it will work itself out
while our mind is immersed in its thought of God. After all
destiny is as insentient as the body and thus has no power
over the mind unless the mind has fallen an abject prey to
its own thoughts and emotions, like that of the common man.

3.   "Siva made over all His possessions to Vishnu and went
     roaming about in forests, wildernesses and graveyards,
     living on begged food. He found non-possession to be
     higher in the scale of happiness than possessions. The
     higher happiness is freedom from anxiety — anxiety over

how to protect the possessions and how to utilise them, etc."                                                               225

*Note*: This is not to be taken as advice to us to imitate Siva, namely, to smear ourselves with ashes, live in cremation or burial grounds and on begged food, in order to gain happiness; for then, cemeteries would be more full of the living than the dead, and there would be more beggars than begged-ofs. We have only to draw the moral that possessions are not conducive to peace of mind, as it has been illustrated in the last text by the case of the Maharani, who had come in search of peace.

Moreover, we must not take this story literally. Lord Siva is Parameswara, the Lord of Kailas, the Supreme Yogi who Himself confers Bliss and *jnana* on His devotees. Where is the necessity for Him to give up anything to gain *jnana* and happiness, He the born *Jnani*? With or without possessions He is Supreme Bliss itself. This surrender of His possessions to Vishnu is a play, a piece of acting to teach us a lesson in renunciation, which alone leads to eternal happiness, just the reverse of accumulated wealth.

Furthermore, merely giving up possessions does not confer happiness, if the mind continues to run amok and creates difficulties for itself far worse than do possessions. The mental attitude towards riches and the world has to change.

4.    "If happiness is due to one's possessions, then it should increase and decrease proportionately to their increase and decrease, and becomes nil if one has nothing to possess. But is this true? Does experience bear this out? "In deep sleep one is devoid of possessions, including one's own body; yet one then is supremely happy. Everyone desires sound sleep. The conclusion is that happiness is inherent in one's own self and is not due to

external causes. One must realise his Self in order to
open for oneself the store of unalloyed happiness."   3

*Note:* This is plain common sense. The happiness of sleep is
patent to all. We call it rest, which is another word for
comfort, for peace, notwithstanding the fact that we are
then completely denuded of all possessions, including our
body. This bliss of sleep is the most precious heritage of
life: man, animal or plant, which have no property or wealth
of any kind. It is a bliss which does not come from any
external circumstance or condition, but from within oneself
— one's own being. This truth is open to every thoughtful
person to verify for himself, and does not require much
strain to arrive at.

5.   "What is happiness? Is it inherent in the Self or in the
object, or in the contact between the subject and the
object?"
Bhagavan: "When there is contact with a desirable object
or memory thereof, and when there is freedom from
undesirable contacts, or memory thereof, we say there is
happiness. Such happiness is relative and is better called
pleasure. But we want absolute and permanent
happiness. This does not reside in objects but in the
Absolute. It is peace free from pain and pleasure — it is
a neutral state."   28

*Note:* Peace, which characterises true happiness, is neither
pain nor pleasure; for both are active states, resulting from
the contact of the subject with the object, as well as from the
memory of it, which requires the going out of the subject
from himself in pursuit of the object, whereas peace is
inherent in the being of the subject himself, as we have
proved it in the illustration of sleep. This peace has no relation
whatever to the object, the not-being. To BE is peace, is bliss.

Happiness is thus always present as our very self. We have only to *be* — not *to think* or *do* — in order to be in eternal bliss. For thinking is always connected with a sense-object — the body, or other bodies, — and never with the Self. Pleasure, being the result of this contact, must perforce be transient, whereas bliss is of the being or Self, the changeless, fixed subject, who is the thinker of all thoughts, the doer of all actions, and the same at all times and in all circumstances.

6.  "There is a state beyond our efforts and effortlessness. Until it is realised, effort is necessary. (This is the state of samadhi, which is blissful). After tasting such bliss even once, one will repeatedly try to regain it. Having once experienced the bliss of peace, no one would like to be out of it, or engage himself otherwise. It is as difficult for the *Jnani* to engage in thought as it is for an *ajnani* to be free from thought. Any kind of activity does not affect a *jnani*; his mind remains ever in eternal peace."    141

*Note*: "Effort and effortlessness" are action and inaction, beyond which stands the state of being, to realise which, efforts of meditation, that is, *sadhana* is necessary. Once the bliss of this state is tasted it can neither be forgotten nor abandoned. In other words, once we transcend the activities of the mind — thinking, feeling, etc. — we will always thereafter endeavour to transcend them in order to taste again the blissful being, till we attain permanency in the latter. Then thinking will be as difficult to perform as it is in the beginning difficult to suppress, with the result that we will remain ever in peace, irrespective of what we do and do not do. This is the *sahaja samadhi* state of the *Jnani*, which is undiluted bliss. Even his action is considered to be inaction because it is effortless.

7.  "The universe exists on account of the 'I'-thought. If that ends there is an end of misery also. The person who is in

sleep is also now awake. There is happiness in sleep but misery in wakefulness. In sleep there was no 'I'-thought, but it is now while awake. The state of happiness in sleep is effortless. We should therefore aim to bring about that state even now. That requires effort."      222

*Note*: Bhagavan persists in hammering in us the truth that happiness comes only from the Self. Whenever there is the thought of oneself — of 'I' — there is also a thought-world — you, they, he, and a million other things, — and whenever there is a world there is suffering. This may be taken as an inflexible law. The world is therefore a state of misery, One who is in utter misery drugs or drinks himself to sleep, so that he may forget himself and his misery for some time in the blessedness of sleep where there prevails freedom from thought and, thus, from misery. After sleeping off his suffering, the drugged person wakes up to resume it again.

Therefore *in order to be perennially free from suffering we have to perpetuate our sleep, even in the waking state*, in the very world itself. This is the aim of all yogic practices and is called *samadhi, which means sleep in the waking state*, or *sushupti in jagrat*, to which all efforts have to be directed.

8.    The pet squirrel is waiting for an opportunity to run out of its cage. The Master remarks: "All want to rush out. There is no limit to going out. Happiness lies within and not without."      229

*Note*: The Master loves to indulge in analogies drawn from everyday life, and this one is apt and beautiful. The squirrel is the *jiva*, which escapes from its "home" — the Self or Heart — to enjoy the pain and pleasure of the world of diversity, although it means homelessness, of being a stranger abroad.

"All want to rush out" applies to the vast majority of people who prefer to be deluded by the world's shadow-show than remain at "home" in its peace and stillness.

The pet squirrel is a baby-squirrel, which the Ashram has kept in a cage to protect it from the marauding cats. Baby squirrels who accidentally fall from their nests on the trees and remain helpless and in the lurch, would be taken up by Bhagavan who would look after them, till they were fully grown up and could look after themselves, when he released them.

9. "Soul, mind, ego are mere words. These are not real entities. Consciousness is the only truth. Its nature is Bliss. Bliss alone is — enjoyer and enjoyment both merge in it. Pleasure consists in turning and keeping the mind within; pain in sending it outward. There is only pleasure. Absence of pleasure is called pain. One's nature is pleasure-bliss." 244

*Note*: Consciousness, Self, Being are one and the same reality. As we have already seen, the Self is blissful: we, in our nature, are bliss, but when we "rush out", to use the metaphor of the last note, when we extrovert and take the body for ourselves, giving it a special name, we become other than ourselves — the body and its name — then we are not bliss. We take upon ourselves the suffering which the body of Mr. So-and-so is heir to. In other words we imagine ourselves the not-Self and likewise imagine in ourselves the suffering and pain of the not-Self. Extroversion is the cause of this false imagination. Instead of looking inwardly at the pure and blissful seer of the world, we look outwardly at the misery and disease-laden world and at the perishable body of the seer, which we mistake for the seer himself.

"Soul, mind, ego are mere words: consciousness is the only truth." This is a timely reminder that we should not lose ourselves in sounds that convey no sense at all. Bhagavan is supremely practical. Nobody knows what soul or ego is, although we repeat the words mechanically, but everybody knows what awareness is, what consciousness and unconsciousness mean, for we daily see before our eyes people in an unconscious state — in sleep, swoon, or under anaesthesia. Therefore the Master uses the word consciousness for the Self and for all its synonyms — soul, spirit, mind, knowledge, intelligence, and even ego, which is a misnomer for the Self.

10.  "Your nature is happiness. You say that this is not apparent. See what obstructs you from your true being. It is pointed out to you that the obstruction is the wrong identity. Eliminate the error. The patient himself must take the medicine to cure his illness. If, as you say, the patient is too weak to help himself, then he must remain quiet, giving a free hand to the doctor. That is effortlessness."                                        295

*Note*: The first half of this text has already been dealt with. With reference to the patient and the medicine, the questioner had pleaded having "placed himself unconditionally in the hands of the doctor". It stands to reason that the Guru cannot see the Self on behalf of the disciple, for he is always seeing it on his own behalf. It is the disciple's mental outlook that has to change and himself to take the medicine prescribed by the Guru in order to remove the false identification. It will not do to plead weakness and go scot-free from the obligation of doing *sadhana*, for anyone can do the same and exempt oneself from making efforts. Bhagavan suggests that if the disciple is "too weak" to make the effort [himself], then he must completely surrender to the Guru. This alternative seems to please most of these "weak" seekers, because it releases them from the necessity of straining themselves. The question now is whether this weak disciple is strong enough to surrender. If he is unable to make a little effort to concentrate his mind, whence will he have the strength to make the far greater effort of surrender, which necessitates constant remembrance? If the questioner has abandoned himself so "unconditionally", as he thinks he has, he would not come to beg for Grace, but would himself be the one to confer Grace, namely, a Guru. In the next dialogue we shall hear Bhagavan's own view on this point. I am giving the whole dialogue as it is in the original to clarify the above points.

Beginners must, however, take heart from the fact that whatever effort they make in this line, it is never wasted: everyone has to pass through all the stages on this path to become *adhikari*, as every man has to pass through infancy, childhood and adolescence to mature into adulthood.

11. Q. May I have Guru's Grace?
A. Grace is always there.
Q. But I do not feel it.
A. Surrender will make one understand Grace.
Q. I have surrendered heart and soul. I am the best judge of my heart; still I do not feel the Grace.
A. If you have surrendered the question would not have arisen.                                                                 317

*Note*: That the questioner is serious as well as determined, no one can deny. He has also "surrendered heart and soul", of which he is "the best judge". Then why is Grace keeping him in the lurch? Is Grace partial, or the Self heartless? We have either to suspect the wisdom and goodness of the Self, or the completeness of the surrender. And as the former is unthinkable, the fault must lie with the latter.

Bhagavan's concluding answer that if the surrender has taken place the request for Grace "would not have arisen", exposes the illusion under which most people who lay claim to surrender, labour, notwithstanding the addition of "heart and soul" into the bargain. Self-analysis, the most scrupulous and honest examination of one's motives and the secrets of one's heart and mind, is a very essential part of our *sadhana*, auxiliary to the *vichara* and *dhyana*. It eliminates all the delusions of the seekers. Persons are even known who imagine that if they use a persuasive language with the Guru they can get from him whatever they want. Self-examination eradicates this foolishness, and sobers them to a sane outlook about the role of the Guru in relation to the disciple.

12. "Every person seeks happiness but mistakes pain-associated pleasure for happiness. Such happiness is transient. His mistaken activities give him short-lived pleasure. Pain and pleasure alternate in the world. What is it that is not followed by pain? Man seeks it and engages in it. To discriminate between pain-producing and pleasure-producing matters and to confine oneself to the happiness-producing pursuit only is *vairagya* (dispassion)."     302

*Note*: Is the end of this text a good definition of *Vairagya*? Not usually in its course, but certainly in its results, Renunciation is happiness. There exists no such thing as happiness in the world, because the world is the not-Self, the Self, as we have already proved it, alone being undiluted happiness. It is a contradiction to seek a virtue or quality in its opposite, say, love in hatred, peace in fear, light in dingy darkness, etc. To expect happiness in an area which is hostile to happiness, namely, the world, is a vain expectation. Yet the activities of all men are based on this false expectation, although they imagine themselves in possession of its fulfilment. This auto-intoxication is like the intoxication of the opium-eater, who drugs himself to an artificial bliss. Yet the Self incessantly asserts itself, and every now and then, through hard knocks, matures a person to the realisation of his deplorable state. This is the *vairagi*, the budding *mukta*, who aims at curing himself of the habit of opium-eating.

13. "The desire for happiness is a proof of the ever-existent happiness of the Self. Otherwise how can desire for it arise? If headache were natural to human beings, no one would try to get rid of it. One desires only that which is natural to him. Happiness, being natural, it is not acquired. Primal bliss is obscured by the not-Self, which is non-bliss, or misery. Loss of unhappiness amounts to gaining of happiness. When misery is eliminated the bliss which is ever-present is said to be gained. Happiness mixed with misery is only misery." 619

*Note*: Much of this text has already been discussed. The first line is very suggestive. That every living being desires its own wellbeing is axiomatic; for it is an innate instinct — inherent in life itself, which ultimately leads to the rediscovery of oneself as eternally blissful.

If happiness is our very Self, as the text declares, how, one may ask, do we then happen to be in this world so devoid of it as to need taking so much pains to gain it? The answer is that we are at no time devoid of it: it is now and has always been present, as our very being. But, Bhagavan avers, this "primal bliss" has been obscured by the apparently enjoyable world which the senses have created. The external objects, the not-Self, being very attractive, have monopolised our attention and have lured us away from the perception of it. Yet enjoyment mixed with misery is nothing but misery. Eliminate the creation of the senses and the unmixed blessedness will stand revealed. There is no need to strive for happiness as such, but strive to do away with the artificial delights of the world, which are misery in essence, to be in perpetual bliss. This is the main point of the text. "Loss of unhappiness amounts to gaining of happiness."

The statement that "one desires only that which is natural to him" does not mean that because one desires a thing, that thing is proved to be one's nature, for that would put a different complexion on the teaching. What it means is that if bliss is not our very existence why should we desire it so ardently? It also means that even the common desires we possess aim at happiness for the Self.

> 14. "Why should there be suffering now?"
> Bhagavan: "If there were no suffering, how could the desire to be happy arise? If that desire did not arise, how would the quest of the Self be successful? What is happiness? Is it a healthy and handsome body, or timely meals and the like? Even an Emperor has endless troubles, though he may be healthy. All suffering is due to the false notion 'I-am-the-body'. Getting rid of it is *jnanam*."      633

*Note*: There you are: pampering the body with all possible amenities — health, the best of food and care, wealthy leisure, good looks, and physical graces, etc. — does not confer happiness: if anything it multiplies the difficulties for a number of obvious reasons. Moral health alone, irrespective of material amenities, leads to tranquillity; for it entails a good deal of dispassion for the body. Hence the more we reduce our attention to and clinging love for the body, the nearer we draw to the bliss of the Self. This is a standing refutation of the belief that the body is our Self and an eye-opener to those who on the one hand desire peace of mind and on the other worship their body more than they do the image of God.

Is suffering an unmitigated evil? Bhagavan answers in the negative. It is on the contrary a blessing, in that it brings us to our senses and compels us to think profoundly and start a quest for liberation from suffering.

The three points which this text proves beyond doubt therefore are: (1) the body is not the man, (2) man is sorrow-less by nature, and (3) sorrow, being an infliction, can be eradicated only by self-knowledge.

CHAPTER TWO

# LIFE, DEATH, AND REBIRTH

1.  News of someone's death was brought to the Master. He
    remarked: "Good. The dead are indeed happy. They
    have got rid of the troublesome overgrowth — the body.
    The dead man does not grieve. The survivors grieve for
    him. Do men fear sleep? On the contrary they court it
    and on waking up they remark that they have had a
    happy sleep. Yet sleep is nothing but temporary death.
    Death is a long sleep."                                    64

*Note*: Bhagavan points out the glaring contrast in our
behaviour in the twin states of death and sleep, which are
the same except in matter of duration. Of that too we cannot
be very sure. We hate death, but run with might and main
after sleep, so much so that if we remain sleepless for a few
nights, we seek medical help and start swallowing sleeping
tablets, if not also resort to drastic morphia injections. In the
temporary death we call sleep, we spread our beds and look
forward to it, singing with the Ancient Mariner:

> "O Sleep, it is a gentle thing,
> Beloved from pole to pole
> To Mary Queen the praise be given,
> She sent the gentle sleep from heaven
> That slid into my soul!"

In the long sleep we call death, instead of feeling happier
still for the departed beloved who enjoys it, we put on long

faces and mourn. The irrationality of our behaviour would appear ludicrous to the man of wisdom but for the poignancy of the intense grief and terrifying fear which death inspires. The Master perceives the body as a "troublesome overgrowth" because it is superimposed on him — the pure being. Though he has a body he sees himself bodiless — *videha*. The body-'I' sense does not exist for him, yet the needs and diseases of the body continue to be "troublesome". The *Videha* is a *Mukta*, sometimes called *Videhamukta*. Devotees worship him as the manifestation of the pure Brahman, but the unintelligent call his state 'living death'. But then we are all working for this 'living death', and they who ridicule him too.

The Master continues:

2.   "If a man dies while yet alive he need not grieve over another's death. One's existence is evident with or without the body. Then why should one desire the bodily shackles? One should find out his immortal Self and be happy."                                                              64

*Note*: In the last note we have seen who the "man who dies while yet alive" is. Naturally such a man does not mourn the death of anybody; for he knows their state and condition as he knows his own, and laughs with joy. Bhagavan speaks from experience when he says that one remains the same under all circumstances and conditions "with or without a body."

3.   A great devotee of Bhagavan lost his only son — three years old. The next day he and his bereaved family came to the Ashram. The Master seeing them said: "Training of mind helps one to bear sorrow and bereavement with courage — the loss of offspring in particular. Grief exists only so long as one believes oneself to be of a definite

form. If the form is transcended one would realise oneself
to be eternal, having neither birth nor death. That which
is born is only the body."                                    80

*Note*: "Transcending the form" is a grand idea. What
death destroys is only the form, and so long as we attach
ourselves to the form we continue to feel the sting of death.
But if by knowledge we come to realise that the form is not
the person we love, we will be able to transcend grief and, in
fact, death itself.

We are all agreed that the beloved is not a mere shape,
a coloured picture, an inanimate substance, but a being, an
entity which teems with life and intelligence, which thinks,
feels, loves, wills, acts, and with which we establish
relationships as father, son, husband, neighbour, friend, etc.
The body, being devoid of intelligence, can, by itself, perform
none of these functions, and, when life (i.e., the man)
withdraws from it, it remains an effete matter fit for
cremation.

The "mental training", which Bhagavan suggests, will
not only kill all sorrow at bereavements, but will also reveal
to us the truth of our immortality, and thus save us from
future birth and death. Hence the Scriptures (*Srutis*) lay down
the law that any perceivable and conceivable object is the
object of consciousness, and thus insentient, changeable and
destructible. The subject or consciousness alone is sentient,
changeless and indestructible.

4.   "See how a tree, whose branches are cut grows again. So
     long as the life-source is not affected it will grow. Similarly
     the *samskaras* sink into the heart in death: they do not
     perish. They are reborn. Just as a big banyan tree sprouts
     from a tiny seed, so the wide universe with names and
     forms sprouts forth from the Heart."                    108

*Note*: This is the rationale of rebirth. The *samskaras*, or impressions, left over at the close of one life become the seeds for the next. They are stored up in the Heart, from which a new body with new environments, new circumstances and new tendencies "sprouts" forth at the right time to form the new life. As the tortoise withdraws its limbs into its shell, so do the lifelong (psychical) impressions gather together at the last moment and, along with the senses, withdraw into the centre of consciousness, to form the nucleus of the future birth. The *Bhagavad Gita* puts this graphically:

"When the Lord acquires a body and when He abandons it, He seizes the senses and *manas* and goes with them, as the wind carries perfume from flowers.

"Enshrined in the ear, eye, touch, taste, smell, and the mind, He enjoys the objects of sense.

"The deluded do not perceive Him when He departs or stays or enjoys, swayed by the qualities (*gunas*); the wisdom-eyed perceive Him."

(XV. 8-10)

Thus the Lord equates the *jiva* with Himself, for it is He, the immortal and changeless, who takes bodies to enjoy the senses through them, discards them, and takes new ones, etc. This is a scriptural confirmation of our immortality and divinity.

With the rise of the body, the senses and all the psychical faculties also rise and spread a universe in infinite space and infinite time. Therefore the whole universe has its roots in the small cavity we call Heart.

5. "If a person we love dies, grief results. Shall we avoid grief by loving all alike, or by not loving at all?"
Bhagavan: "Both amount to the same thing. When all have become the one Self, who remains to be loved or

hated? The ego that grieves must die. That is the only
way."                                                    252

*Note*: We have already discussed the point that he who
grieves is he who takes the body for the beloved himself.
When the body dies the beloved himself is believed to have
died. Who is responsible for this error? The ego, of course,
that is, the person who mistakes himself for his own body.
But this ego is itself an erroneous conception, an imagined
entity. The conclusion is therefore clear that the whole
phenomenon is dud — the dead, the grief over the dead,
and the one who is stricken with grief over the dead. It is an
incubus created by the imagination, of which it is difficult to
rid oneself. If a way can be found to kill the incubus, say, by
a *sadhana*, the hallucination will disintegrate of its own accord
into the reality of the Self. In that case the love to which the
questioner refers will have no occasion to manifest, because
of the absence of duality of lover and loved, the Self being
the sole existence.

6.   "You ask if it is the ego that reincarnates. Yes, but what is
     reincarnation? The ego is the same but new bodies appear
     and hold it. Just observe what happens even (now) to your
     body. Suppose you want to go to London. You take a
     conveyance to the docks, board a steamer and reach London
     in a few days. What has happened? The conveyance travelled
     from one part of the world to the other. The movements of
     the conveyance have been superimposed on your body.
     Similarly the reincarnations are superimpositions. Do you
     go to the dream world, or does it come to you? Surely the
     latter. The same may be said of the reincarnations. The
     ego remains changeless all along."                      311

*Note*: The main point of this text is that what happens to the
individual rises from inside himself, though it appears to come

from outside. Birth is the assuming by the individual — *jiva*
or ego — of a body woven from inside himself, like the dream
body which rises from the dreamer himself and superimposes
itself on his mind, or what is the same, himself. This is the
meaning of "Do you go to the dream, or does it come to you?"
Death is the temporary elimination of that superimposition,
and birth is the reestablishing of it in a new form, and so on
and on till *jnana* brings the superimpositions to a radical end.
This resembles the infinite number of webs which the spider
spins out of himself for his temporary use.

The analogy of travelling demonstrates the fact that the
individual himself remains always the same, and that the
long journey (*samsara*) is not undertaken by him but by the
number of vehicles he uses for the purpose. The *jiva*
constructs its own vehicles (bodies) and rides them for its
own pleasure, as it were, according to the demand of
*prarabdha* — the result of its behaviour and its psychical
impressions in its use of the previous bodies. It is therefore
wrong to say that we die and are reborn, or that it is we who
go round and round on the wheel of evolution. We remain
always the same without beginning or end. Let us fix that
firmly in our mind lest we lose ourselves in Darwinism,
Occultism, Behaviourism and the rest of their tribe.

7.  "Do intellect and emotions survive death?"
    Bhagavan: "Before considering that, first consider what
    happens in your sleep. Sleep is only the interval between
    two wakings. Do these survive in this interval? They
    represent the body-consciousness and nothing more. If
    you are the body they always hold on to you. If you are
    not, then they do not affect you. The one who was in
    sleep is the one who is speaking now. You were not the
    body in sleep. Are you the body now? Find out this, and
    the whole problem will be solved.

"That which is born must die. Whose is the birth? Were
you born? How do birth and death affect the eternal Self?
Think to whom these questions occur and you will
know."                                                    426

*Note*: This is extremely interesting to those who are interested
in their own death. You are awake now, and you will be
awake tomorrow. But in between the two there is a gap of
no-waking state. What happens to your intellect and
emotions in that state? You may plead ignorance of what
happens, but you *do* know that you exist then, otherwise
you would not mention the gap, namely, sleep, at all: you
would not say "I slept for six hours last night," admitting
thereby that you undergo the experience of sleep as you
undergo that of waking. If there were an interruption in
your existence at night, you would end with every day and
be a new man every morning. Then there could be no
question of your being able to remember that you met so-
and-so yesterday, or did such and such thing twenty years
ago. There would be no memory of anything previous to
this day, not even of your name, home, business or family
relationship at all, for it would be as if you had taken a new
birth. The fact that the memory of previous incidents, objects
and of having again and again slept and wakened persists,
proves your fixity, that you are a logical continuum, passing
through a variety of experiences, sometimes pleasant and
memorable, and sometimes the reverse. You are the thread
on which all these experiences string themselves, like beads.

   "Granting," you may contend, "that I exist in all these
experiences and states and in all these years, how is it that I
remember most of these experiences, but not those which
happened only a few hours ago in my sleep?" The answer is,
we are not concerned with the experiences at all; for memory,

like the senses, returns to the Source in sleep and comes out
again on waking. We are concerned only with your own
existence and, as you admit its continuity in sleep, there
remains nothing for us to do but to apply this to the state of
after death. I think there should be no difficulty to do that.
Taking our stand on the continuity of the *jiva* even in the
absence of the body in sleep, we find that the possession of a
body need not be the criterion for existence. That being the
case, what valid evidence do we have to postulate extinction
of existence with the extinction of the body? Certainly none.

As for our intellect and emotions after death, they will
go where they are even now going every night.

Bhagavan's remarks now become obvious: "The one who
is in sleep is now in waking. You were not the body in sleep,
so you are not it now. That which is born — the body —
must die. You are not born so that you may die. Births and
deaths do not affect you — the Self."

8.   "How were we all in our previous births? Why do we not
     know our own past?"
     Bhagavan: "God in His mercy has withheld this
     knowledge from people. If they knew that they were
     virtuous, they would grow proud; contrariwise they
     would be depressed. Both are bad. It is enough that one
     knows the Self."                                      553

*Note*: The question comes from the Ashramites: it occurs in
fact to almost everyone in the spiritual line. Bhagavan rightly
thanks merciful God for causing this oblivion before rebirth,
or else the world would have been in complete chaos, and
life far more miserable than it is already under the present
conditions. Apart from the pride or humiliation, of which
Bhagavan speaks, there are thousands of events and things
which are better completely forgotten, and millions of people

who had better remain unrecognised for one's own sake and for the sake of the people concerned. Problems would have arisen in such numbers and of such a nature as to make the earth too hot for a decent man to live in. We have therefore to say "sufficient unto the day is the evil thereof", and offer thanks to God Almighty for drawing a heavy curtain between one life and another.

Yet we have all heard of some "occultists", who claim the power to rend the curtain and see the Past, and wonder what good has that done? Has it given *jnana* to the person whose past life is supposed to have been read, or even to the "occultist" himself? If it does anything at all, it is to create serious doubts of its genuineness in some minds, and an abject, primitive faith in some others, both of which are definitely spiritually harmful. Why, therefore, dabble in useless preternatural matters? Bhagavan reminds us that the only knowledge worth acquiring is that of the Self: the rest is pure fantasy.

9.    "Where is the necessity for reincarnation? The theory of evolution is physically perfect. But for the soul further development may be required which happens after death."
The Master: "Let us first see if there is incarnation before we speak of reincarnation. Who is the man: the body or the soul? You answer 'both together'. But you do not cease to exist in the absence of the body, say, in sleep. You call sleep temporary death. Therefore life is also temporary. If life and death are temporary, there must be something which is not temporary: *that* is the Reality. See for whom these questions arise. Unless the questioner is found, the questions can never be set at rest."    644

*Note*: Doubts about past births have been expressed by many people, more especially by those whose scriptures do not teach reincarnation. The questioner is a Muslim who has found complete satisfaction in the theory of evolution without the necessity of rebirths and without deviating from his theological beliefs, except in that man has sprung up from the amoeba. But his questions carry in them their own solutions, if they are but carefully thought out.

In the first instance he admits the immortality of the soul and its continued development after death till perfection is achieved, yet he is unable to rid himself of the bias for the body, which he makes the partner of the soul in the synthesis of his self, or 'I'. On what ground does he give the body a place in the make up of the 'I', he does not care to investigate. If the body is half his self, then this is no longer a homogeneous unit, but a hybrid compound of mortal and immortal substances, of which the immortal, which he calls the soul that survives death, is only a part, or half. Is this rational? Moreover, if the soul is not an integral whole, how is it possible for it to attain perfection in the evolution of which he speaks? Again, how does he know that the soul undergoes "further development" after death? What does he, first of all, conceive the soul to be to require this development? Confusion becomes more confounded when he gives the body a share in his 'I', endowing it with sentience, with intelligence, when a little thinking would have convinced him to the contrary. By admitting mortality to the body, he has at once confessed to its insentience, for sentience never dies: it is eternal life. The body is thus insentient and therefore unintelligent; whereas the 'I' is pure intelligence as the knower of all things. Therefore the body is neither the 'I' nor a part of it.

As for rebirths, why does he find them illogical? If in this life he is born, as he admits he is, why cannot he be reborn? That which has caused this birth should be a valid cause for another birth. What makes him imagine that the cause of this birth of his has exhausted itself and can no longer be available for another birth, or a series of new births?

Let us illustrate this by a concrete example. A man marries because he has a desire for a woman. If the woman a little later dies, he may marry a second time, impelled by the same urge. But suppose he also loses his body in the meantime, what is he to do to satisfy this persistent craving? Naturally he has to take another body, as he had taken the present one for some desire or other.

Thus Bhagavan tells us that there is no such thing as rebirth: what there is, is only assuming one body after another for the satisfaction of desires. If you do not want to take another body, by all means you are at liberty not to, provided you have ceased to crave for anything, thereby eliminating the cause of "rebirth".

We have therefore to study man before we enquire about evolution, reincarnation, life, death, etc., which is what makes the Master advise the questioner to discover himself first.

Bhagavan continues:

10.  "One sees an edifice in his dream. Then he begins to think how it has been built brick by brick by so many labourers and during so long a time. So also with the theory of evolution. Because he finds himself a man he thinks that he has evolved from the primal state of the amoeba."                                    614

*Note*: This makes our sciences dream sciences. So they are. It is a well-known fact that scientists do not concern themselves with the absolute reality, which they leave to the philosophers to do, and remain satisfied with the physical reality, for example, the splitting and multiplication of the chromosomes, the proportional combination of the hydrogen and oxygen atoms to form the water molecule, etc. And when they step out of the physical into a non-physical area they get confused and confounded. When biologists, for example, speak of the evolution of life, they really mean the evolution of the form which the life inhabits, as we see before our eyes the evolution of the human body from the pinhead zygote to the size of the newborn babe, to that of childhood, adolescence, and full adulthood, and the gradual unfoldment of the mind in it. Scientists do not have direct contact with life to know what life is, whether it evolves or remains changeless. They cannot, for instance, directly perceive the life in the chromosome but can only infer it from the behaviour of the chromosome, whose physical qualities they can directly observe: size, colour, shape, movements, changes, constituents, etc.

Therefore those who believe in the laws of evolution must understand that their knowledge is very partial, and pertains only to the insentient universe, which alone can be perceived and can suffer changes.

As life is a closed book to the scientists, so also is life's other name — mind. Not their activities, but life and mind as they are in themselves, as substances, as 'First Principles'. If they knew the nature of the mind, they would have also known that all their endeavours were limited to a world which is essentially a dream, taking place inside their own consciousness. For at no moment can the scientist step out of his mind and say 'here is a real world which can stand by itself without me — without my mind'. When one is in a dream and is asked to step out of it to realise that it is a dream, one can shake oneself a bit and be out of the dream to the waking state to verify his old position. But in the waking dream — *jagrat* — it is not so easy, because the senses are then all out, fully entrenched in this their own dominion, of which they are the absolute monarchs. This is the reason why the scientist refuses to believe himself dreaming, and continues to imagine that he had crawled out of the amoeba into the monkey some millions of years ago, and out of the monkey some scores of thousands of centuries ago. How are we to convince him of his error that it is not he who has undergone all these metamorphoses, but the shapes of the bodies he has assumed? If he could be convinced of this truth, he would presumably be also convinced that the amoeba, the monkey, and the millions of years are parts of the evolution of this, his *jagrat* dream.

# CHAPTER THREE

# DESTINY AND FREE WILL

1. "Can destiny (karma) ever come to an end?"
   Bhagavan: "Karmas carry in themselves the seeds of their
   own destruction."                                          11

*Note*: Karma is the destiny created for oneself by one's free
actions. In actions are included thoughts and sensations,
motives, good or bad emotions, etc. While working out an
old destiny one is bound to create a new one by the manner
in which one reacts to its operation. Here then comes the
place of free-will. We are not free to alter the trend of an old
karma, for example, in the choice of our parents, country,
the circumstances of our birth and environments; of our
physical and mental fitness and abilities. These are forced
on us: we cannot change them. What we can change is the
manner in which we receive and work them out. We are all
agreed that there are many things in which the decision lies
in our hands: the decision is ours, the action is ours, the
motive behind the action is ours, the mental attitude with
which we do the action is ours too. This then is the field in
which we are allowed freedom of will, and it contains the
seeds of our future destiny. We can shape that destiny as we
will, and if, like most people, we are not aware of this truth,
we allow ourselves to be carried away by our impulses and
eventually land in worse trouble than we are in already. Most
often the new karma does not follow on the heel of the one

which is being worked out now, so that we drag the chain of our slavery through several lives.

Here the salutary precepts of the Scriptures come to our rescue to make us rectify our views on life and our attitude towards others. These and the persistent knocks of destiny gradually soften our impulses, modify our outlooks, sharpen our intellect, and slowly but surely turn us into seekers; then into yogis; and finally into full-fledged *Jnanis*, when karma ceases. *Jnana* totally annihilates it. Let us not forget that all these improved changes or evolution — take place not in the man himself, but in the faculties which are superimposed on him, that is, in his views and actions.

*Jnana* is thus brought about by a good karma, generated by a good free-will, which is the result of persistent suffering from a bad karma, generated by a bad free-will. Karma is like an inanimate machine, which yields up what you put into it. That is why the Master begins his *Upadesa Saram* with the statement that karma is *jada*, insentient, unintelligent. What makes it move and act as stern destiny is the energy generated by the exercise of our free will.

It may be asked that if a persistently bad free-will caused by the embitterment resulting from a persistently bad karma brings about a worse karma, which drags us down and down, where is the chance of our ever coming up to the surface again? We must not forget the saving Grace of suffering and the inherent purity of our nature, which will not permit us to remain forever insensible to degradation and misery: we cannot forever remain sunk in bottomless ignorance and never attempt to climb up to freedom. Suffering and the intense urge to return to ourselves act as floats and buoy us up from the depths of this vast ocean of *samsara*. Thus the action of karma through suffering gives the impetus to *jnana* which destroys karma.

This is what Bhagavan means by "karma carries in itself the seeds of its own destruction."

It goes without saying that karma takes effect only in a physical body; for a debt incurred in a physical body has to be paid also in such a body, either in this very body or in a future one. The Vedanta does not believe in an after-death payment; hence rebirth is necessary.

2.  "Even without any initial desires there are some strange experiences for us. Wherefrom do they arise?"
    Bhagavan: "The desires may not be there now. But they were once there. Though forgotten they are now bearing fruit. That is how the *Jnani* is said to have *prarabdha*. Of course this is so from the point of view of others who observe the *Jnani*." 115

*Note*: The questioner seems to think that people are always conscious of their moral delinquencies, of their sins of omission and commission, of the effect of their actions upon others, as well as of their own desires. They are not: excessive greed and lack of consideration for the feeling and interest of others, are, unfortunately, a common malady, as witness politics, competition in business, and a hundred-and-one other deliberate and otherwise daily lapses in their conduct towards their neighbours. So to play the injured innocent for the troubles they get, cannot cheat Providence. Unconsciousness or oblivion of old desires, old sins and actions which affected oneself and others in this life or in previous lives, does not cancel the poetic justice that is necessary to restore the disturbed balance. Even the *Jnani* brings his destiny from another life, but this works itself out without creating for him a new karma, or a new birth, or causing him anguish, as do the same troubles to others. His mind, having totally sunk in the Self, has become, under all circumstances, as fresh and cool as summer moonlight. Others, seeing the suffering of his body, imagine the *Jnani* himself to be suffering.

3.    "As long as you feel yourself the doer of action so long you are bound to enjoy its fruits. But if you find out whose karma it is, you will see that you are not the doer. Then you will be free. This requires the Grace of God, for which you should pray to Him and meditate on Him."                                                    115

*Note*: Desires lie at the root of destiny. We desire and move to acquire its object. Then we never think of the identity of the actor, our whole attention being centred on the object till we secure it. The question of doership in the light of truth and untruth does not occur to us at the moment. Enjoyment of the object preoccupies us most, enjoyment which we tacitly accept as the reward for our action, for our endeavour to gain it. This is karma done with a sense of doership, the doer being the empirical 'I', even if the sense is not actively in the mind: it is implied in the act itself, and thus binds us.

Now, if we investigate into the cause and motive of the action and into the nature of the actor, we will find that he who has acted with the motive of enjoyment is not the real 'I', but an imitator, a false 'I', then we shall be automatically released from the responsibility of the action, and thus from the bondage of karma. Although we henceforth act, the sense that it is we who are acting drops from us, and with it also drops the power of karma to grip us; for the empirical 'I' will no longer be there to be gripped.

But this discovery or realisation, does not come without the help of God, or Self, Bhagavan asserts, through intense worship and meditation. We shall hear more of this in the following Chapters.

Bhagavan continues the explanation:

4.  "Action without motive does not bind. Even a *Jnani* acts and there can be no action without effort and without *sankalpas* — motives. Therefore there are *sankalpas* for everyone. But these are of two kinds, the binding (*bandha-hetu*) and the liberating (*mukti-hetu*). The former must be given up and the latter cultivated."  115

*Note*: Here is a way out of the karmic stream. Bhagavan postulates action for all men, and results for all action, yet repudiates the binding residue of action to apply equally to all actors. Action binds only to the extent that its motive element is of the binding type, the *bandha-hetu*, and never if it is of the liberating type, where the material, selfish motive, is totally absent. Therefore, those who wish to jump out of the stream of bondage into that of liberation have to curb their binding *sankalpas* and cultivate those of *mukti*.

The question may now be asked — How are they to distinguish between the two, which is admittedly difficult to do? This text is mainly meant for the *sadhaka*, who constantly worries whether a certain action of his is consistent with his *sadhana* or not. Bhagavan dissipates this doubt by admitting action to all men, and a motivated action too. For example, in olden days Bhagavan himself used to work in the kitchen, and even once built a mud wall to his cave on the hill. He knew then why he did that work, and certainly aimed at the utility element in it, or else he would not have done it. But when Bhagavan worked he was all along aware of his true being as the doer of the action, which is desireless. The motive of this action is thus not of the binding type. Therefore the *sadhaka's* action should not worry him, so long as it is not of the binding type, having desires in the background.

5    "Free will and destiny are ever existent. Destiny is the
result of past action; it concerns the body. Let the body
act as may suit it: why are you concerned with it? Why
do you pay attention to it? Free-will and destiny last as
long as the body lasts. But *jnana* transcends them both."

193

*Note*: "Free-will and destiny are ever existent" is a significant
statement which belies those who attribute to Bhagavan
himself the self-contradictory theory that no free will exists,
but only karma which predetermines every action and every
experience through which we pass, even the most trifling.
It goes without saying that karma cannot exist without free-
will. It is only free action which attracts rewards or
punishments, i.e. karma, so that free-will and karma rise
and fall together. That karma concerns the body and that
we should therefore let the body act as it chooses, requires
some explanation.

Karma and free-will are, like the body, insentient, and
can affect only the body, and never the intelligent being
who operates it and who transcends them both. Therefore,
so long as the body-'I' sense prevails, they continue to
function and the *jiva* continues to take one body after
another for the working out of karma; but as soon as *jnana*
dawns they cease to bear fruit. Karma will end with the last
body (of the *Jnani*) and free-will will no longer be the will
of the *jiva* (which usually decides on the body-'I' basis) but
that of Brahman into which the *jiva* has now completely
merged.

Therefore, Bhagavan advises the seeker to pay no
attention to the working of karma on the *uphadhis*, but to
dissociate himself from them, when he will be free from the
obligation of taking new bodies, and consequently from
bondage.

6. "So long as there is individuality, one is the enjoyer and doer. But if it is lost, the Divine Will prevails and guides the course of events.

"Free-will is implied in the scriptural injunctions to be good. It implies overcoming fate through wisdom. The fire of wisdom consumes all actions and wisdom is acquired through *sat sanga* — the company of sages and its mental atmosphere." 209

*Note*: All the Scriptures recommend good action, admitting by implication the freedom of the will; for if the will is not free, where is the point of asking us to be good? Man would then be like a machine or an animal which is not responsible for its action and thus cannot be punished. The fire of wisdom here means the power of discrimination which the company of the wise stimulates. Discrimination between good and evil, of necessity induces us to choose the good and shun the evil, the ultimate results of which will be the cessation of doership — not the action itself, but the sense of our being its doers, which implies the merging of the individual will in the Divine Will, as of the individuality itself in the Divine. Thenceforward "the Divine Will will guide the course of action."

7. "When *prarabdha* karma gets exhausted, the ego completely dissolves without leaving any trace behind. This is final Liberation. Until then the ego continues to rise up in its pure form even in the *Jivanmukta*. I still doubt the statement of maximum duration of twenty-one days." 286

*Note*: This is an answer to a statement supposed to have been made by a great saint of the last century that, according to the questioner, "*Nirvikalpa samadhi* cannot last longer than twenty-one days" or death results. This, on the very face of it, is inadmissible. What the Sage probably had in mind and, as it often happens, wrongly reported, was the ceaseless stay in *samadhi* with total unconsciousness to the world for twenty-one days, for it might have been considered impossible for the body to last longer without nourishment. Even this cannot be right. Total unconsciousness to the world never takes place in the true *samadhi* (See XIII, 48), for it would cease to be *samadhi* and would become *sushupti* (deep sleep). What lasts for long durations and is mistaken for *nirvikalpa* is a simulation of it, a sort of a cataleptic trance called *laya*, resembling the profoundest sleep and swoon, where total unconsciousness of the Self as well as of the world takes place, contrary to the experience of *nirvikalpa*, where the Self as Pure Consciousness reigns supreme and alone. This cataleptic state can be brought about by the practice of *kevala kumbhaka*.* We hear of coma-like trances of long durations, which have nothing to do with the true *nirvikalpa*. The same also happens to some beginners who let themselves go in meditation and unwittingly slip into *laya*, which they either mistake for *samadhi* or remain baffled, not knowing what to make of it.

Moreover, if this statement of twenty-one days were true, there would have remained no one to teach the truth. All the Rishis of the Upanishads and all the great *muktas* of whom we have heard, would have been in their graves before anyone had heard of them, and before they had time to instruct anybody. Besides, there would have been nothing for them to instruct — the experience being one of deep sleep, if total unconsciousness to the world is the meaning of the statement. Even the Vedas would not have seen the light of day.

---

* *Vide* Appendix

Bhagavan avers that the body falls out only after the exhaustion of its karma, and not before. We also know that in many cases it lasted forty, fifty, or even more years after the attainment of *sahaja nirvikalpa*. Bhagavan's own case is a shining example of it. He entered *videhamukti*, the final disembodied Liberation, after having remained for fifty-four years in unremitting *nirvikalpa*. Till then, Bhagavan tells us, the ego continues to pop up, even for the *jivanmukta*, but in its purest form, that is, without causing the *Jnani* ignorance of the reality and the suffering consequent on this ignorance. What it may cause him is a temporary, superficial belief in the reality of the world due to the intense impact of the senses, hence it is called ego, *though pure*.

8.  "It is not enough that one thinks of God while doing karma (service, or worship), but one must continually and unceasingly think of Him. Only then will the mind become pure."
    Bhagavan's attendant then remarked: "Is it then not enough that I serve Bhagavan physically, but must also remember him constantly?" To which Bhagavan remarked: "'I-am-the-body' idea must vanish through vichara." 337

*Note*: The attendant is right in interpreting Bhagavan's remark. Seeing the Master physically comes nowhere before the contemplation of him with the mind. Yet service to him has its great utility, in that the very close proximity to his person has tremendous potentialities for the purification of the attendant's *vasanas*, due to the utter purity of the Master's mind. But that is not sufficient to give *mukti*. Purificatory processes are only a stage on the path, to make one fall in the line of mental practices — *dhyana* and *vichara*, — which alone can prepare the mind to experience Brahman in the last stages of the long journey. "'I-am-the-body' idea must vanish through *vichara*," Bhagavan asserts.

The path of service is the path of surrender, which is not limited to time and space; for it is round the clock and round the equinoxes process. It goes on for years of remembrance — a mental process again — of God, Guru or Self.

9.  "Your idea of will-power is success insured, whereas will-power should be understood as the strength of mind which meets success and failure with equanimity. It is not synonymous with certain success. Why should one's attempts be always attended with success? Success develops arrogance and one's spiritual progress is thereby arrested. Failures on the other hand are beneficial, inasmuch as they open one's eyes to one's limitations and prepare him to surrender himself. Therefore one should try to gain equipoise of mind under all circumstances. That is will-power. Again success and failure are the results of *prarabdha* and not of will-power. One man may be doing only good and yet prove a failure. Another may do otherwise and yet be uniformly successful. This does not mean that the will-power is absent in one and present in the other."    423

*Note*: The context is the case of a man, who, because of repeated reverses in business, has lost confidence in himself, and who is now trying to find a way of recovering it. He is confusing confidence with will-power. One may have abundant confidence in oneself, yet the will to work is lacking. The case of the questioner is the reverse of this, namely, he has the will to work, but is pessimistic about the results of his labour, on account of persistent failures in the past. Bhagavan advises him to develop an equal attitude to both success and failure, which after all depend on one's destiny, at the same time he praises failure as more spiritually fruitful in the long run than success, in that it kills arrogance and promotes an attitude of *vairagya*, which hastens one's approach to the supreme goal. Most people live in abysmal ignorance of their glorious destiny; more so of their weak points — of their *tamasic* and *rajasic* cravings and behaviour. The rich in particular take the strongest objection to these being pointed out to them in a direct manner. How, then, can God open their eyes and save them from this self-intoxication? He gives them disasters and calamities to shake their airy castles and crack the thick crusts of their arrogance. Pride of wealth, of position, fame, power, learning and, worst of all, of lineage eventually destroys itself, crushing down over the head of its owner to his everlasting good.

# CHAPTER FOUR

# SIDDHIS AND VISIONS

1.  "Is not making oneself invisible (like Vasishta and Valmiki) evidence of advanced Wisdom (*jnana*)?"
    Bhagavan: "No; for in that case all those who have spent their lives in the sight of others would be considered *ajnanis*. It might have been the *prarabdha* of these sages to develop these powers (*siddhis*) side by side with their *jnana*. Why should you aim at that which is not essential, but on the contrary is apt to prove a hindrance to *jnana*? Does the sage feel oppressed by the visibility of his body? A magician can render himself invisible in a trice. Is he a *Jnani* for that? Visibility and invisibility imply a seer. Who is that seer? Find him out first. Other matters are unimportant." 30

*Note*: What counts most is *jnana* — the knowledge of Truth. This is called Realisation of the Absolute, or Realisation of the Self. The *siddhis* are not the Self itself, but its powers, as are seeing, smelling, thinking, etc., with the sole exception that the latter are common experiences, whereas the *siddhis* are not. The powers themselves are unintelligent: the intelligent is their possessor. To fix the attention on the powers and not on their owner, who is the reality, is, therefore, like throwing away the pearl and retaining its shell.

Again, as the common perception is a hindrance to *jnana*, so are the *siddhis*, only more so, because the latter are apt to slacken one's efforts towards the Highest, and make him fall prey to the wealth and fame which follow them like their shadow. Therefore *siddhis* are far more dangerous in the pursuit of Brahman than the senses. They are condoned only if they are accompanied by *jnana*, as is the case with Valmiki, Vasishta, and others. They have no spiritual value whatever in other cases, and their use cannot but be highly detrimental to him who uses them and him — the weak-minded — who is taken in by them.

2. "The disappearance from sight by yogis like Vasishta and Viswamitra concerns only physical matter. Is that our chief interest? Are you not the Self — the Reality? Why trouble yourself about extraneous matters? Take the essence and reject other theories as useless. Those who imagine physical invisibility counts in the quest for *mukti* are mistaken. No such thing is necessary. You are not the body: what does it then matter if it disappears in one way or another? There is no great merit in such phenomena. Achievement of the Real alone matters. The loss of the ego is the main object, and not the loss of the body. Identity of the (real) Self with the (unreal) body is the real bondage." 31

*Note*: Sadhana, that is, search for the Absolute, consists of mental and spiritual purification through certain yogic practices. But *siddhis* have reference only to the body, to make it appear and disappear at will; to make it hear things in a manner not usually heard, or see things in a manner not usually seen, or smell things in a manner not usually smelt, and so on. In other words, *siddhis* take one in a diametrically opposite direction from that which the keen yogi should take. We reject the ways and habits of the body in order to have our attention fixed on the soul, which uses the body and which is the one, eternal reality, whose attainment completely redeems us from the bondage of the flesh and from sorrow and ignorance. *Siddhis*, as it has been demonstrated in the last note, perpetuate *avidya*, often degrade and strengthen the ego, which we are out to destroy. Consider the tremendous popularity and deification of the 'clairvoyant' and 'clairaudient', and the power he wields over the superstitious, the credulous, the feeble-minded, who would by far run after this *siddhi*-exhibitor rather than after the man of truth who has attained complete union with God, and who is in a position to show the direct way to this truth and its bliss. We have also to consider the very frequent possibility that the *siddhis* not being of the genuine brand.

Bhagavan calls them "extraneous matters", totally irrelevant to the true seeking — "there is no merit in such phenomena." The true *siddhas* are the *Jnanis*, who do not preach *siddhis*, and scarcely ever exhibit them. On the contrary, they teach nothing but the science of the Absolute and the way to It. They have nothing to do with *koshas*, creation, life-after-death, mental and astral planes, fairies, ghosts and the like. The reality cannot be intuited with all this lumber filling every corner of the head. Fairy tales, if taken seriously, bar the way to the reality of Brahman; certainly, real *adhikaris* do not indulge in them.

Bhagavan continues:

3.   "Leave off false notions and perceive intuitively the Real. That alone matters. If you melt a gold ornament what matters how it is melted, whole or in parts, or of what shape the ornament had been? You are only interested in the gold. Realise the Self."      31

*Note*: When we buy gold we do not question what shape it had before it was melted, and how it was melted, etc. Similarly we should not waste our time on how we are born and how we die, how many spheres and planets we had visited, if we did visit at all, and who we were in our past lives. All this is dross, superfluous curiosities, "false notions," which we have to "leave off ". What we want is the gold, namely, to *know* and *be* ourselves. If this is gained the riddle of the universe is solved. The universe of the "clairvoyant" is romantic even if the clairvoyance is genuine. What it sees is as false as dreams, as false as this waking state, which we aim at transcending rather than preoccupy ourselves with. The dreamer is alone real — the dream total hallucination. The seer is the gold, the seen the dross. The Self of the seeker is the reality, and to this Self we should direct our whole attention.

4. "With Self-realisation real and incessant *tapas* results. With the maturing of such *tapas* some *Jnanis* can make their bodies intangible and invisible. These are known as *siddhas*." 57

*Note*: This is very important to note. *Tapas* does not mean here the austerities that precede Realisation, but the inherence in the Self after Realisation. *Ramana Gita* says in this connection: "He who is fixed in *sahaja* state is in automatic and incessant *tapas*." (XI, 18) Again: "The pristine nature of the Self is effortless, spontaneous *tapas*. Incessant *tapas* of this kind leads to the manifestation of all powers." (XI, 24) This immediately draws a clear line between a *siddha* Rishi and a "clairvoyant", a magician, or a miracle-worker whom we sometimes meet in this country and who have no *jnana*, as it is shown by the display of their trade far and wide and by their superficial teaching, if they have any.

5. "People look to the body only and want *siddhis*. They are not content with the idea of *jnana* and so want *siddhis* to be associated with it. They are likely to ignore the supreme happiness of *jnana* and aspire for *siddhis*. For this they are

going through the by-lanes instead of the royal path,
and so are likely to lose their way. In order to guide
them aright and keep them on the royal road alone,
*siddhis* are said to accompany *jnana*. In fact *jnana*
comprises all, and a *Jnani* will not waste a thought on
them. Seekers must try to get *jnana* and then seek *siddhis*
if they so desire."                                          57

*Note*: The main purport of this text has already been discussed
in this chapter. The people who are attracted to *siddhis* are
the ones who have a great attachment to their bodies, for
whose sake they seek *siddhis*, ignoring the real blessedness of
*jnana*. These people are their own enemies. The statement
that *siddhis* accompany *jnana* to "guide them aright and keep
them on the royal road" is noteworthy. The exhibition of
*siddhis* is permissible only on the condition that it brings the
straying sheep back to the fold — the "royal road" of *jnana*
or Truth. There is nothing more unpleasant to the
Enlightened man than the sight of people being led away
from the right path by exhibitionism, by a glamorous display
of the "miraculous". To the *siddhi*-'fans' Bhagavan gives a
way to gain true and sound *siddhis*, namely, by first trying to
acquire *jnana* and then work for *siddhis*, if they will continue
to long for them. Then they will have a healthy appraisal of
*siddhis* and their use.

6.  "In *Halasya Mahima* there is a chapter on the eightfold
    *siddhis*. There Siva says that His *bhaktas* never waste a
    thought on them. Again Siva says that He never grants
    boons. The desires of the devotees are fulfilled according
    to their *prarabdha* only. When *Ishwara* Himself says so,
    what of others? In order to display *siddhi* there must be
    others to recognise it, which means that there is no
    *jnana* in the person who displays *siddhis*. Therefore these
    are not worthy of any thought. *Jnana* alone must be
    aimed at."                                                57

*Note*: This evidence of Siva against *siddhis* must be taken very seriously. For here He is in His highest Form, as the Supreme Yogi, the Spirit and Soul of the universe, which is Pure Consciousness and Bliss. The Tantrikas, the Kaulas in particular, aim at *siddhis*, which they mistake for the highest spiritual achievement, and their Master and Giver of *siddhis* and of all boons is this very Siva with His consort Devi, also called Bhairavi. The *jnana*-seeker takes the former Siva as his ideal and guide; hence His repudiation of *siddhis* and boons in *Halasya Mahima* is of great significance to him.

The other noteworthy point refers to boons being granted only on the basis of merits, that is, according to the individual *prarabdhas:* they are not fortuitous, as they are commonly mistaken to be.

The third point deserves close attention. What Bhagavan means by the display of *siddhis* requiring the presence of others to witness them, which automatically brands the displayer as *ajnani*, is that the *Jnani* is ever in the Self, cognising nothing but the pure Consciousness which alone exists — one without a second. To exhibit *siddhis* implies the admission of multiplicity, which *jnana* negates. The deliberate displayer of *siddhis* thus stands a self-confessed *ajnani*,* the *Jnani-siddha* mentioned before is excepted.

7. "*Atma* alone is to be realised. Its realisation holds all else in its compass: *shakti, chakras, ganapati, siddhis*, etc. These are included in it. Those who speak of these have not realised the *Atman*." 57

---

* "O Lord of Munis, only he who has no *atmajnana* and is not liberated seeks *siddhis*. The liberated One never follows *avidya*. *Siddhis* can never help the attainment of the seat of *Paramatma*." (*Varaha Upanishad*).

*Note:* This affirms the previous texts. Bhagavan, being concerned only with the Absolute takes his stand on the following truth: all things, all powers, all phenomena have a common source which must be changeless and eternal. This absolute Source goes in the Scriptures by various names, of which the best is *Atman* or Self, which is easy for everyone to comprehend, being represented by one's own existence, or being, which everyone loves and is aware of. Therefore the Self is the repository of all powers, all shapes, all colours, all thoughts, all sensations — the whole universe, physical, emotional and mental, in brief. The knowledge of the Self is consequently alone true knowledge, true enlightenment, because it is perennial and all-inclusive. These its manifestations or emanations are unstable and thus cravings for them lead to ignorance and misery. Those who deal with *siddhis, chakras, shakti,* psychic phenomena and the like, Bhagavan says, have proved themselves to have not beheld the light of Truth, and should thus be shunned. Let us note this very carefully.

8.    "A Swiss lady, while sitting before Bhagavan with her eyes wide open, saw the Master's face becoming cherub-like and draped in glorious flowers. She was drawn in love towards that childlike face. She described the vision to Bhagavan. He remarked: 'The vision is in your own mind. P. B. saw me as a giant, you saw me as a child. Both are visions. Do not be deceived by them. P. B. had his eyes closed, whereas you had your eyes open. Probably you had been thinking of a child, and it came in your vision.' The lady confessed that she had, namely, the childlike face of Siva."          304

*Note:* "Do not be deceived by visions" is a scriptural injunction. The extent of unreliability of visions can be gauged by the discrepancy between the vision of P. B. which recorded a giant figure and that of the lady which recorded a mere child for the one and the same person. All visions are psychosomatic, mostly emanating from the subconscious, as this lady has confessed to a prior thought of the childlike Siva. They need not all be as obviously known to the subject himself or herself as this vision, or its origin, has been known to the lady in question. Some subjects do expect and look forward to visions, and so they have them. They cook up their visions inside themselves and then see them with closed or open eyes, outside them. God has been the greatest victim of such hallucinations. He who is changeless, formless and only one, and the same for all nations, has been made to appear differently to different people, which has cost many million innocent lives and has brought incalculable suffering to many more living millions. The Greeks saw Him as Zeus, the thunder-wielder, Jesus conceived Him as a Father, and His followers later expanded Him to "Three-Persons-in-One-God". To Moses He appeared as "I-am-that-I-am", which Bhagavan often quotes. To the Hindus He is Rama, Krishna, and many others. Yet He is the One and only Being who resides in all hearts. *Ajnana* cannot be better demonstrated than in the intolerance and bigotry, which conventional religions have exhibited in the recorded history of man. This shows the danger of taking visions and symbols for truths and acting on them.

Bhagavan continues:

9. "Visions are not external. They appear only internally. If external they would assert themselves without there being a seer. In that case what is the warrant for their existence? The seer only." 305

*Note*: Is the vision independent of the seer? We know that it is not. Then how can it be real? The reality must be self-sufficient, substantive, wholly depending upon itself, and must be present at all times. But visions are not only temporary, but also depend on the qualities and abilities of the mind of their seer. Therefore all visions are false.

10.   "Many visitors here tell me that they get visions or thought-current from you. I am here for the last month and a half and still I have not the slightest experience of any kind. Is it because I am unworthy of your Grace? If so, I feel it disgraceful that I, being of the lineage of Vasishta, should not have your Grace, while far off foreigners should have it. Will you kindly suggest what expiation I should suffer or undergo to remove this disgrace?"
Bhagavan: "Visions and thought-currents are obtained according to the state of the mind, which depends on the individuals themselves and not upon the Universal Presence. Moreover, they are immaterial. What matters is peace of mind."                                                   317

*Note*: I have recorded here this item, not so much for the Master's answer, which has been substantially recorded earlier, as for the quality of the question. This illustrates my previous statement that visions often come to those who expect them. This questioner has been expecting a vision since six or seven weeks, and its absence has made him miserable, because he is suspecting his own spiritual worth — he, a direct descendant of the great Vasishta Muni. To be ignored in favour of "foreigners" who are of no lineage worth speaking of, of no caste whatever, is a disgrace to him, an extremely puzzling calamity.

One feels for the poor man's grievance indeed. But is this a genuine grievance? He does not seem to heed the persistent teaching of the Master, made in his very presence, that visions are rubbishy stuff, and that not lineage but *adhikara* alone counts in this path. I have brought this out as a specimen of the mental outlooks of the worshippers of *siddhis* and the harm these do in perverting the mind. Had this gentleman extended his experience a little longer in the Ashram, he would have found men who had lived there not for six *weeks* but for six, ten and fifteen years and yet had had no visions of any kind, and had not felt thereby any slight to their lineage, their personal dignity, or spiritual advancement, but who, on the contrary, considered their absence a perfect grace from the Master, amply proved to them in other ways.

The peace of mind of which Bhagavan speaks is naturally contingent on the direct apprehension of the Reality. *That* peace, and not visions, must be our objective.

11.   "It is said of some saints that they revived the dead. Yet even they did not revive all the dead. If that were possible there would be no death, no cemeteries, no world, etc."

342

*Note*: The context is as follows. A mother had brought the body of her dead child about three hundred miles by train to Tiruvannamalai, on which she had paid a very high fare, basing herself on a dream in which she had been told that Bhagavan's touch would revive the child. The corpse was not permitted to be brought inside the Ashram, so that the touch was not granted. But to satisfy the disconsolate, bereaved mother Bhagavan substituted the touch by an oral statement that, if the dream were true, her son would revive on the next day. Thereupon the body was kept for the night and cremated the next day.

Now was that not a cruel dream? But this is the fate of those who shape their lives on dreams, visions, prophesies, ethereal sounds and sights, etc. In all probability this dream had originated from a wishful thinking of the mother.

Bhagavan rightly remarks that even those who were said to have revived the dead were of limited powers, their action being against the course of nature. Otherwise humanity would have attained immortality, but would have thereby created such complications — economic, political, domestic, social — for itself that dead-revivers would have been at a discount, if not also restrained by the law.

Revivals by the touch or the grace of saints must be taken to depend on the *prarabdha* of the revived person, as the evidence of Lord Siva given in text 6 above proves.

CHAPTER FIVE

# BRAHMACHARYA, SOLITUDE AND SOCIAL LIFE

1. "*Brahmacharya* is 'being in Brahman' (or 'living in Brahman'). It has no connection with celibacy, as it is commonly understood. A real *Brahmachari*, that is, one who lives in Brahman, finds bliss in Brahman, which is the Self. Why should he then look for other sources of happiness? In fact emergence from the Self is the cause of all misery."                                                17

*Note*: To be oneself is the most blissful state. That is *Brahmacharya*, or 'living in Brahman'. How then can he who has been so fortunate as to enjoy that bliss seek the much lesser pleasures of the world, which, apart from their being doubtful, depend upon others to confer or withhold? The inference therefore is that celibacy is granted in a *Jnani*, who is ever in the brimful bliss of the Self. Yet this inference will be wrong if it is taken as a general rule that *Jnanis* are always celibates; for some of the most famous *Jnanis* are known to have married one, or more than one wife and have had children, some with possessions and some without. A *Jnani* is a liberated person: liberated also from all rules and regulations; from all codes of ethical, religious and social conduct — he is a law unto himself, and there is no knowing what he does and does not do. Yet he is known to lead a *sattvic* life, having divested himself of all the *rajasic* and *tamasic* tendencies even before the attainment of *jnana*.

Celibacy as a help to *sadhana* is in this Advaitic line doubtful. A married life is, from this point of view alone, certainly no bar to the highest: it may even be of more help in certain cases, in what the Tantras call the '*vira*' or 'heroic' *sadhaka*. In cases where celibacy does not create definite mental and emotional disturbances which mar the peaceful *sadhana*, then certainly it is of great help, inasmuch as it rids one of the preoccupations, duties, and anxieties which a family life drags in its wake. And to make this point clear Bhagavan continues the explanation:

2.    "Celibacy is certainly an aid to realisation among so many other aids."                                                              17

*Note*: "Among so many other aids" must not escape us: It is the main point in this text. It gives celibacy a negligible value on a par with so many other helpful factors. This is confirmed by the next answer.

3.    "Is not then celibacy indispensable? Can a married man realise the Self?"
      Bhagavan: "Certainly, it (Realisation) is a matter of fitness of mind. Married or unmarried one can realise the Self, because the Self is here and now."                                       17

*Note*: The Self is All: the married as well as the unmarried. Being one's own self, who can be debarred from experiencing it in its utter purity, if the mind has been prepared for it? If celibacy is the only cause of eligibility, then all celibates should be *muktas* and all *grihastas* in abysmal bondage, which experience and tradition refute.

4.    "How does a *grihasta* fare in the scheme of *Moksha*?"
      Bhagavan: "Why do you think yourself to be a *grihasta*? If you go out as a *sannyasi*, the thought that you are a

*sannyasi* will haunt you. You will be only substituting one thought by another. The mental obstacles are always there. They even increase in new surroundings. There is no help in the change of environment. The mind is the obstacle. Therefore why change the environment?"

54

*Note*: The real enemy, therefore, of the *sadhana* is not so much a domestic life as the habits, the restlessness, the pet notions, the desires, the stubbornness, the dullness — the immaturity, in brief — of the mind which keeps us company wherever we go. Why blame it on the family, or sometimes even on God Himself?

Bhagavan rubs it in:

5.   "The environment never abandons you, according to your desire. Look at me. I left home. Look at yourselves. You have come here leaving the home environment. What do you find here? Is this different from what you left?"   54

*Note*: "Look at me: I left home", Bhagavan says, forgetting for a moment that what he found in the pitch-like dinginess of *Pathalalinga* (underground cave) in the Big Temple at Tiruvannamalai, to which he had escaped from home in 1896, was entirely different from his home "environment" in Madurai. To strike a personal note of my own, I would add that seeing Bhagavan all day long, and seeing a grasping landlord as an incubus of a neighbour elsewhere, an incubus which certainly was not "according to my conscious desire", makes a Himalayan difference. But we understand what the Master means. One carries one's environment with him, which is not other than one's own mind, as we discussed in the last note. No one can leave his mind behind and go out in search of God. The mind is thus the most troublesome as well as the most helpful instrument, depending on the use

we make of it, an instrument which keeps us constant
company. It makes the environments.

By "the environment never abandons you, according
to your desire", Bhagavan wishes to impress upon us again
the relentlessness of the mental *sankalpas* — our own whims
and fancies, — which shape our circumstances. We thus
prepare our bed and we sleep on it.

6.  "Even if one is immersed in *nirvikalpa samadhi* for years
    together, when he emerges from it, he will find himself in
    the environment which he is bound to have. That is the
    reason why Sankaracharya emphasised *sahaja samadhi* in
    preference to *nirvikalpa samadhi* in his excellent work
    *Vivekachudamani*. One should be in spontaneous *samadhi*,
    that is, in his pristine state, in any environment."      54

*Note*: Bhagavan continues the topic, but includes in the mind
the physical environment, which, for the *Jnani* affects only
the physical body. Even the *Jnani*, Bhagavan elsewhere asserts,
has to be subject to the *karma* of the body — his mind being
no longer tarnishable. The *Jnani* is ever in *samadhi*. When he
switches off the world, he is in *nirvikalpa* (better call it *kevala
nirvikalpa*, because *sahaja* is also called *nirvikalpa*. Vide chapter
on *samadhi*); when he switches it on, he is in *sahaja*, that is,
perceiving the physical world at the same time as being in the
reality, The physical environment of the *Jnani* is chalked out
for his body by *prarabdha*, and this sticks to him as long as he
is in the body. But of whatever sort it may be, it cannot affect
his mind which is ever centred in the "pristine state",
irrespective of what the physical environments are.

7.  "Solitude is in the mind. One may be in the thick of the
    world and maintain serenity of mind: such a one is in
    solitude. Another may be in a forest, but still unable to
    control his mind. He cannot be said to be in solitude. A

man attached to desire cannot get solitude wherever he
may be. A detached man is always in solitude." 20

*Note*: We have already observed that the state of the mind is
the true environment. But the remark of the Master about
the relation of desires to solitude can be summed up as:
"Desire is the crowd, and desirelessness solitude." Or, "Desire
creates the city and desirelessness the forest." Bhagavan
develops this point:

8.   "Work performed with attachment is a shackle, whereas
     performed with detachment does not affect the doer.
     The latter is in solitude even while working. As for
     service, Realisation of the Self is the greatest service that
     can be rendered to humanity. Therefore the saints are
     helpful although they dwell in forests. But it should not
     be forgotten that solitude is not obtained in forests only,
     but even in towns, in the thick of worldly occupations.
     The help is imperceptible, but it is still there. A saint
     helps the whole humanity unknown to it." 20

*Note*: This should give the quietus to the criticism that yogis,
or seekers of the path of Liberation, are selfish. The critics
will now see their short-sightedness in attaching great
importance to physical service, which on no account can give
permanent and all-round satisfaction. Laws of Economics
and Social Reform may work well on the physical plane, may
increase the earning capacity of the labourer, give him a
better shelter, educate his children, and raise him to a higher
social status. But it can never give him happiness. We see it
before our eyes that the more you raise wages, the greater
will be the struggle of the labourer to gain more — he never
knows where to stop his demands. But even if you make
him a millionaire, his mind will remain an indigent
proletariat, like the fuzzy and ever-agitated minds of all the

millionaires under the sun. Therefore all this talk of working for, and uplifting the poor is intrinsically based on false values. Poor is he who is unhappy, even if his wealth were that of Croesus. The greatest wealth is the peace which flows from true knowledge, which can be imparted only by these "selfish" yogis and Rishis. This does not mean that philanthropists and social workers should close shop and cease helping. It is their *dharma* to help, which they cannot shirk, for in the performance of this *dharma* lies their own salvation. But they must stop sneering at the one who alone can give the most valuable help of all, namely, redemption from ignorance and misery — and for ever.

The questioner remarked: "In Europe it is not understood by the people that in solitude one can be helpful, imagining that working in the world alone can be useful." Bhagavan: "Never mind Europe and America. Where are they but in your mind? Realise yourself and all will be realised. If you dream and wake up and recall the men of your dream, will you try to ascertain if these men are also awake?"

CHAPTER SIX

# THE WORLD

1.  "If you make your outlook that of wisdom, you will find
    the world to be God. Without knowing Brahman, how
    will you find His all-pervasiveness?"                    1

*Note*: This 'outlook of wisdom' is that of the *Jnani* who
has realised Brahman which he finds to be the source of all
perception, that is, of the world. Brahman is not only the
source of the world, but also its pervader, nay, its very self
— its warps and woofs, its very stuff and texture. But this
all-pervasiveness of God cannot be perceived till the realisation of the Self has been fully achieved in *Sahaja Samadhi*.
To tell the unrealised person that the world is God is like
writing it on water — meaningless. Ask him first to realise
God, or Brahman, and he will cease to puzzle, but will try
to understand.

2.  "The world is not external. The impressions cannot have
    an outer origin, because the world can be cognised only
    by consciousness."                                       53

*Note*: What is the world? Bhagavan answers, "impressions
in the mind." Do impressions have a source? Modern
psychology answers, "Yes, the external stimuli," which
Bhagavan repudiates. The psychologists have no proofs at
all of a non-psychical stimulus located in outer space. Yogic
experience has shown that there exists no such thing as outer

object or space, for if it were, it would not be known at all:
what is not mental cannot impress the mind. Therefore
impressions rise from the consciousness itself, like the dream
impressions which rise from the dreamer's mind and are
perceived by it. The world cannot stand by itself, but has to
depend upon consciousness to be known, or else how can
we be sure that it exists at all (See X, 10)? If for, example, in
the midst of the dream we are to be challenged to prove that
the world we then perceive and the food we then eat were
only figments of our imagination, we would be in as much a
dilemma to prove it as we would should such a challenge be
thrown at us in the waking state about the *jagrat* world and
*jagrat* food; for, while in dream we take the dream to be real,
much as we take the waking to be real while in it.

3.    "Can the world exist without its percipient? Which is
      prior to the other? The Being-consciousness, or the
      rising-consciousness. The Being-consciousness is always
      there, eternal and pure. The rising-consciousness rises
      forth and disappears. It is transient."                    53

*Note*: Bhagavan follows the line of argument of the previous
text that the thinker, whom he calls the Being-consciousness,
must precede his thoughts, — the world, — which he calls
the rising-consciousness. The thinker must be in existence
before he starts thinking. The thinker is one and fixed,
whereas his thoughts are countless and ceaselessly change.
Thus, the Being-consciousness is the "eternal and pure"
Reality and the source of the rising-consciousness, which is
transient.

4.    "The world is the result of your mind. Know your mind,
      then see the world. You will realise that it is not different
      from the Self."                                             53

*Note*: This sums up the previous texts. The mind projects the world. In order, therefore, to know what the world is by nature, the mind must be looked into. This investigation will ultimately lead to the discovery of the identity of the mind with the Self. So, "see the seer," or "know the knower" is the master-key which opens the grand secret of the Self and the source of the world.

5.  "Is the world perceived after Self-realisation?"
    Bhagavan: "What does it matter if the world is perceived or not? The *ajnani* sees the *Jnani* active and is confounded. The world is perceived by both; but their outlooks differ. Take the cinema, for instance. Pictures move on the screen. Let the pictures disappear. What remains? The screen alone. So also here. Even when the world appears find out to whom it appears. Hold the substratum of the 'I'. When the substratum is held what does it matter if the world appears or disappears?"                    65

*Note*: One sympathises with the questioner: his curiosity is a common weakness. In the beginning of this answer the Master wishes to draw attention to he fact that to the *Jnani* there is neither gain by seeing the world, nor loss by not seeing it. What matters most is the Being, which is the man himself — as he is in himself — self-sufficient and perfect, and in this Being the *Jnani* is firmly established. It thus matters very little if he perceives the extraneous world or not.

   To speculate about the mental state of the *Jnani* is an idle labour, for it is anybody's guess, like the state of the Supreme Brahman; for both are one and the same, notwithstanding the appearance of activity on the part of the *Jnani*. This activity is, truly speaking, inactivity, like the movements of pictures on the screen, which in reality do not exist. There is no activity whatever on the screen, but only an appearance of it. As the screen is alone real and the pictures unreal, so is the Self alone real, and not the action. Activity and the world in which it takes place are thus both unreal. The 'I' is the screen, the sentient seer, and all pictures and worlds are the insentient shows playing in, or upon it.

Bhagavan asserts that when you are confused by the sights, turn your attention upon yourself, their seer. Continue doing that again and again and you can bet on your assured success.

6.   "How to turn the mind away from the world, you say? Is there a world apart from the Self? Does the world say that it exists. It is you who say that there is a world. Find out the Self who says it."     81

*Note*: The substance of this answer is the same as that of the preceding ones, but it differs from them in form. In all fundamental principles we discover unity in the substance but diversity in the presentation, which is the superficial form. Differences in the questions impose differences in the answers, and differences in the spiritual quests are responsible for all the scriptures in the world. Otherwise even the voluminous Vedas could be summed up in one syllable — OM.

Thinking is the world: it creates the world. We think and our thoughts appear as the external objects. That the world had been before we were born and continues to be after we are dead, and that science and history bear evidence to this fact, does not alter the truth that even these scientific and historical facts are our *present* thoughts or notions — notions which haunt us as long as we are in *jagrat*. All the worlds and the billions of ages which they have lasted, tumble down like a pack of cards the moment we lay our heads on the pillow and sail off from *jagrat*, and with them come down the history of the people who preceded us and the world which preceded the people, etc. Yet, notwithstanding the total *pralaya* of our *jagrat* thoughts, the complete blotting out of the universe — in our beds — we continue to BE, to travel to new lands and cross new seas, though lands and seas are, like *jagrat*, our own creation. So the dreamer of *jagrat* is alone real — the *jagrat* dream a total fake.

7. "You say that the world is materialistic. Whether it is materialistic or spiritual, it is according to your outlook. Make your outlook right. The Creator knows how to take care of His creation."    240

*Note*: The last sentence makes us think of the politician, social worker, philanthropist, economic philosopher, and even the clergyman who are ever anxious to help the nation and the world, perpetually thinking of how to save humanity from misery and disaster. Bhagavan practically tells them that there is a power which is making and moving all things: Who are you to imagine that you can make and unmake to your liking? Such worries denote ignorance of Providence, or the arrogation to oneself the duties of Providence. These preoccupations should be abandoned by the seekers, who are expected to begin with a strong faith in the omniscience and omnipotence of the Supreme Being Whom they are seeking. Service of others is only permitted if it is done as a *sadhana* with *jnana* as the ultimate aim, as a means to self-purification. Find truth and all will be well with the world: "make your outlook right, for the world is according to your outlook".

8. "Does Bhagavan believe in evolution?"
Bhagavan: "Evolution must be from one state to another.

When differences are not admitted, how can evolution arise? You say that when Sri Krishna tells Arjuna that after several births the seeker gains knowledge and thus knows "Me", denotes evolution. But you must not forget that the Gita begins with "Neither I was, nor you, nor these chiefs, etc."; "neither it is born, nor does it die, etc." So there is no birth, no death, no present as you look at it. Reality was, is, and will always be. It is changeless."      264

*Note*: The questioner is a Theosophist, and, like Arjuna and Darwin, sees the evolution of forms and mistakes it for the evolution of life, which is changeless. When Sri Krishna saw that Arjuna was unable to grasp His meaning about the absoluteness of the subject, which is neither born nor dies, He turns a leaf and starts speaking a language which Arjuna understands. What moves, changes and progresses is the form which the life inhabits, or its ideas, concepts, outlooks, which are its functions, and not itself as the thinker or conceiver. We have all observed how man daily changes his views about things and the world, from infancy to old age, though himself remains the same *jiva*. Life is changeless and ever perfect, so that it has no need to progress, to "evolve". Life is pure sentience, i.e., eternal existence, which is bound by no frontiers to need breaking its chains through "evolution". It is the usual human astigmatism, rather failure in precision of language that ascribes progress to life and brings in evolution and reincarnation. The Srutis also speak of rebirths, but they know what they are talking about, as does Sri Krishna in the Gita. They say this to the millions of Arjunas of all ages, but speak a different language to the dedicated *sadhaka* who has prepared himself to receive the truth absolute.

9.    "What should we do to ameliorate the condition of the world?"

Bhagavan: "If you are free from pain, there will be no pain anywhere. The trouble is due to your seeing the world externally and also thinking that it has pain. But both the pain and the world are within you. If you look within there will be no pain."                272

*Note*: Here again the world is sitting on our shoulders: its misery is weighing heavily on us: "What should we do to ameliorate it?" Is this true altruism? Is the life of the man who worries free from the blemishes of selfishness? If not, we know the exact value of such altruism. But this is not really the concern of Bhagavan, who approaches the question from the absolute level. You look outside, he tells us, and see a world, and then you start worrying over its suffering. But is the world really there that you should take its suffering so seriously? The whole drama is enacted by, and inside your mind. You are like the thief dressed as a policeman going in search of the thief. The whole show of sympathy and concern for the world is a show put up by the criminal who is responsible for the world and its suffering. The thinking mind creates the world and its suffering, and the thinking mind now poses as the saviour of the world. Bhagavan virtually asks it not to be a hypocrite: Root out your own sins and you will see no sins anywhere.

10.  "Is there a spiritual hierarchy of all the original pro-pounders of religions watching the spiritual welfare of humanity?"
Bhagavan: "There may or may not be. It is only a surmise at best. *Atma* is *pratyaksha* (self-evident). Know it and be done with speculation. One may accept such a hierarchy; another may not. But no one can gainsay the Self."                274

*Note*: I have underlined "It is only a surmise", which should be taken as an authoritative statement from the

Master that no one can have the means of knowing definitely whether such a hierarchy exists or not. This must not be forgotten, so that all such claims may be taken at their face value.

But even if such a hierarchy exists, can it help us to attain the reality? Yet "watching the spiritual welfare of humanity" sounds very attractive. But the question is, suppose this is true, how does somebody's watching from some unknown area in some distant, unknown world over, say, my spiritual welfare, help me to attain the reality — a process which should be undergone by myself alone, inside my own consciousness, through the immediate guidance and presence of a Master, who has himself attained it, and has become the reality personified, and who is far more competent for this job than any invisible, remote "watcher"? It all appears mist and fog to the seeker who is too practical and too rational to hug shadows, "speculative" hypotheses. The path is too simple to admit dubious complications. The truth is self-evident (*pratyaksha*), says the Master. It does not consist in discovering hierarchies, but in discovering the mind, or the being, which discovers hierarchies and everything that is known. And as everybody is a being, it follows that every man is himself the truth and the container of all things, a fact which cannot be "gainsaid". "Know Thyself" remains the wisest and the most practical counsel.

Bhagavan continues:

11. "Anyway there is nothing apart from the Self. Even the "spiritual hierarchy" cannot exist apart from the Self. It is only in the Self and remains as the Self. Realisation of the Self is the one goal of all."                274

*Note*: This clinches the matter: even this hierarchy is, if it does exist, included in that one absolute Self. Then why not seek the Self alone right now? Why waste your time on secondary, irrelevant matters, which will lead nowhere?

12. "A phenomenon cannot be a reality simply because it serves a purpose. Dreams also serve dream purposes; for example, the dream water quenches dream thirst. The dream creation is however contradicted in the waking state. What is not continuous cannot be real. The real is ever real, and not real once and unreal at other times. The same is with magic, which appears real yet it is illusory. Similarly the world is not real apart from the reality which underlies it." 315

*Note*: This is an answer to some Tantrikas who hold that the world is not an illusion like a mirage, because it serves a purpose which the mirage does not. Bhagavan refutes the argument of utility as a criterion of reality, on the analogy of dream-objects which have their utility in the dream world, e.g., dream fire cooks dream food, and dream food satisfies dream hunger, and so on, yet they do not exist. The test of reality is not utility but perennial continuity, which places the phenomena of this world — of *jagrat* — on a par with those of dreams, being as ephemeral and, therefore, as illusory as them, whereas Reality is the fixed substratum on which the phenomena appear. The dream's substratum is the dreamer himself. The *jagrat* dreamer is the substratum of the *jagrat* phenomena. He is real but not the phenomena; and as the dreamer of dreams and of *jagrat* are the one and the same *jiva*, the *jiva* is therefore the Absolute Brahman, which once again validates the identification of the *jiva* with Brahman by the Srutis: "*jive Brahmaiva na parah*" (there is no difference between the *jiva* and Brahman).

The next text graphically illustrates this point.

13. "There is fire on the screen in a cinema show: does it burn the screen? There is a cascade of water: does it wet

the screen? There are tools: do they damage the screen?
Fire and water are only phenomena on the screen of
Brahman and do not affect it."                    316

*Note*: This is a practical and perfect illustration of Sri
Krishna's words in the *Bhagavad Gita* that fire does not burn
it (the Self), nor does water wet it, nor can swords cut it, of
which no one can plead ignorance; for there is scarcely an
intelligent person who has not witnessed it in a picture-house,
and has not known that the piece of cloth — the screen —
which receives the fury of fire, water and swords remains
completely unaffected by the celluloid conflagration that
appears to rage on it. The screen is the seeing mind, the
subject spoken of in the last note, and the celluloid
conflagration is the world.

14.    "Why should individuals remain caught in the affairs of
this world and reap trouble in the result? Should they
not be free? If they are in the spiritual world they will
have greater freedom." The Master answered: "The world
is only spiritual. Because you identify yourself with the
physical body you speak of this world as physical and
the other world as spiritual. Whereas that which is, is
only spiritual. If you realise yourself as the spirit, you
will see that this world is only spiritual."           328

*Note*: If pure consciousness alone is, the phenomena
that are seen and endured by it are utterly superfluous. But
because we take them seriously, we say that the affairs of the
world are troublesome. What is more serious is that we take
the body to be even more real than the phenomena, because
the body adheres to us throughout life as an inseparable
companion, from which we have no relief. We are never
given a chance in the waking state to see ourselves by
ourselves without the body, so that we may distinguish

between the real us and the unreal body. This ceaseless companionship through which we perceive, act, obtain and enjoy the objects of our desires, has created the illusion that the body is our very Self. And in that illusion lie all our difficulties. Because the body is physical, we think that we are physical; because the body is diseased and tired, we think that we are diseased and tired, and so on. But when the Master draws our attention to our error, we take measures to correct it — from seeing the outer world, including the body, we turn back upon our own selves as the knowers of the world and the body; for knowledge is not physical: it does not have shape, smell or colour; it cannot be bound by time or limited by space, as does the body. We will thus realise ourselves to be the infinite Consciousness which uses the body, when the suffering of the body will cease to affect us, and we likewise will cease to see the world and the body as external, but as phenomena inside our own Self. From being physical the world will turn out to be consciousness or spiritual in essence. The conscious separation of the body from the pure consciousness, as a first step, will thus resolve all doubts and is the aim and object of this *sadhana*.

15. A Spanish lady writes in a letter: "If the individual self merges in the universal Self, how can we pray to God for the uplift of humanity?"
Bhagavan comments: "They pray to God and finish with, 'Thy will be done.' If His will be done why do they pray at all? It is true that the Divine will prevails at all times and under all circumstances. The individuals cannot act of their own accord. Recognise the force of the Divine will and keep quiet. Each one is looked after by God. He has created all. You are among 2,000 millions. When He looks after so many will He omit you?
"Again there is no need to let Him know your needs. He knows them Himself and will look after them." 594

*Note*: The recorder adds that "the question seems to be common among the thinkers of the West." So it is! for the simple reason that the Westerners are taught from infancy to pray for others, not forgetting, of course, to begin with themselves, their fathers and mothers, sisters and brothers. At the same time they are taught to have absolute faith in the Lord. They find no inconsistency in having this absolute faith side by side with ordering Him to execute what they wish Him to, as if He knows nothing about it. They forget the Sermon on the Mount which enjoins them, like this text, "Be not ye, like unto them (the heathens who make long petitional prayers): for your father knoweth what things ye have need of, before ye ask him" (Matthew VI, 8).

Sometimes they even involve God in international squabbles and invoke His help on both sides of the fighting line. They coerce Him through mass religious processions and open-air prayers.

Rational faith is a great unifying force in the spiritual world, but blind faith is most disastrous all around, as the lurid history of the Dark ages has evidenced. Blind faith is still going strong in this 20th century, but, mercifully, with all its fangs blunted.

Followers of Sri Ramana remain consistent and hold on to the rational Advaitic path. God is our very Self, and so long as we do not realise Him as such, we continue to bear this belief firmly in us, which we reinforce by the conviction that no man is ever neglected. God, Who is infinite wisdom, knows what is best for each and does it without our reminding Him. He does not need our suggestions or advice.

Bhagavan continues:

16.   "Still more, why do you pray? Does not your Creator and Protector know that you are weak? You say God helps

those who help themselves. Certainly, help yourself and
that is itself according to God's will. Every action is
prompted by Him only. As for prayers for others it looks
so unselfish on the surface of it. But analyse the feeling
and you will detect selfishness there also. You desire
others' happiness so that you may be happy. Or you
want the credit for having interceded on others' behalf.
God does not require intermediaries. Mind your business
and all will be well."                                      594

*Note*: Bhagavan's accusation of the intercessor of selfishness
is fully justified. We have only to read religious history to
realise the havoc this intercession played in the political,
social, domestic and spiritual life of the West. Intercessions
and certificates of intercessions under the name of indul-
gences were bought and sold in the open market for some
centuries in Europe, and the practice, at least the notion of
intercession, still, even today, lingers among a vast section
of humanity, so that we should not wonder at people who
want to pray for others and for the peace of the world and
pose as heroes in the eyes of God and men. Even in India
the imported notion has spread to some spiritual institutions, where intercession is being practised on a large scale.
Bhagavan reminds us that "God does not require intermediaries."

That "every action is prompted by God" requires some
explanation. On the face of it, it looks as if this statement
negates karma and free-will. In fact it does not. What it means
is simply this: since the Self or God is pure intelligence, that
is, alone intelligent, and since no action is done without an
intelligent actor, it follows that the Self Itself is the doer (or
prompter) of all actions, notwithstanding these being bound
by the laws of karma, which are themselves the work of the
same Self. Thus God is the all-doer and all-knower.

The Self alone is intelligent existence, and because it is not perceived as such, there is all this wrong thinking, this false belief about the impotence, sinfulness and ignorance of man, which need confessions, intercession of saints, prayer for forgiveness and for peace, and what not. Bhagavan shows us the right way and asks us to mind our own business and go on practising till we realise the truth about God and about humanity by our own efforts and direct experience.

17. "Does not God work His will through some chosen person?"

Bhagavan: "God is in all and works through all. But His presence is better recognised in purified minds. The pure one reflects God's actions more clearly than the impure mind. Therefore people say that they are the chosen ones. But the chosen man does not himself say so. If he thinks that he is the intermediary, then it is clear that he retains his individuality and that there is no complete surrender."                                              594

*Note*: That God is alone the doer we have already discussed the point. The new point brought in here is to the effect that only a pure mind can understand Him as such, and such a mind does not pose as intercessor. He who so poses, as certainly many people do, should be branded as victim to egoistic delusions.

But the questioner seems to mean differently from the implications of deliberate intercession. He seems to refer to an act of Divine Grace for the benefit of someone or other, or of a whole nation, through a human agency. This is quite valid. But Bhagavan's point is that such an agency is possible in a mind which is fitter than another for this particular work. Yet this 'chosen' person would not know, still less say, that he is chosen without contradicting his mission, for the simple reason that the choice is an automatic act, and appears to the person himself as natural as any other act, though it turns out to be for the benefit of mankind.

If we grant that all actions are God's then there is nothing to distinguish one act from another, all actions being induced or inspired by the intelligent actor from inside himself without the reminder that it is God's. The same may be said of the universally or individually beneficial act. Thus he who poses as an intercessor, a conscious intermediary, must be looked at with suspicion, more so if he lays claims to higher spirituality through the *tapas* of surrender. This proves that his surrender is very defective and his *tapas* not worth the name.

18. "Are not the Brahmins considered to be the priests or intermediaries between God and others?"
Bhagavan: "Yes, but who is a Brahmin? A Brahmin is one who has realised Brahman. Such an one has no sense of individuality in him. He cannot think that he acts as an intermediary." 594

*Note*: This definition of Brahminism is as ancient as the hills. When Bhishma was lying on his bed of arrows some thousands of years ago and taught the Dharma Shastras to the Pandavas in the presence of Sri Krishna, he also, like Bhagavan, gave the true meaning of Brahminhood, as follows:

"Acts alone determine who is a Brahmana and who is not. Performing all rituals and sacrifices does not make a Brahmana. There is only one bondage, namely, that caused by desire. He who is free from this bondage is a Brahmana. He who restrains his senses, who is constantly in yogic *samadhi* is a Brahmana: he is distinguished above all others, and derives his joys from the Self alone." (Shanti Parva of the *Mahabharata*)

Thus a Brahmin is, truly speaking, a dweller in Brahman, a *Jnani*, or at least a foremost *sadhaka*, irrespective of his physical descent. But the questioner is thinking only of the sacred-thread wearers, who claim Brahminism by right of descent, which the Srutis, Smritis, as in the above quotation, and Bhagavan repudiate. Yet the Brahmins as a caste have done a lot of good to India and to the world by saving the Shastras from destruction, through staunch adherence to tradition in the many vicissitudes through which this subcontinent has passed in its long history. But unfortunately, the wind of change that blew over the world in the last century or two affected this caste also. The majority of the Brahmins found themselves faced with the need to struggle for their existence, which compelled them to occupy positions which had been reserved for the Kshatriyas and Vaishyas. Yet, notwithstanding these disadvantages they continue to stand in the forefront where the study and practice of Yoga and Vedanta and the spreading of Sanskrit knowledge are concerned, which is a redeeming feature in the materialistic tendencies of this age.

It is now clear that there exists no human agency of any kind that can intervene between God and man. The *Jnani*, the God-realised *mukta*, alone can help — not as intermediary, but as teacher of, and guide to, the absolute state of the Self.

19. "Dream and sleep do not make any appeal to me. The sleep state is really dull; whereas the waking state is full of beautiful and interesting things."
Bhagavan: "What you consider to be filled with beautiful and interesting things is indeed the dull and ignorant state of sleep to the *Jnani*. (A Sanskrit saying goes) 'The wise one is wide awake just where darkness rules for

others.' You must certainly wake up from the sleep which
is holding you at present." 607

*Note*: The English lady who has asked this question seems to
have unwittingly given us the secret of Creation. She has
most probably hit on the cause of the disturbance of the
*gunas* in consciousness, which has given rise to the senses,
that is, the world. The disturbance is admittedly an inner
impulse, an urge to experience the "beautiful and interesting
things", and lo! the beautiful and interesting things *are*. The
formless, colourless, tasteless, smell-less, soundless state of
the pure being becomes intolerably 'dull', and the stir in
consciousness takes place to spread a dream, to erect a
picture-house in order to enjoy a kaleidoscopic show, this
world of multiplicity. At all events the desire of this lady for
beauty, is the cause of this body of hers, which permits her
to enjoy "beauty".

Now the question arises, if the questioner is so devoted
to the beautiful things of this world, why does she leave hem
daily to seek the "dullness" of sleep? She is hardly consistent
in her loyalty to beauty when she deliberately and even
longingly forsakes it for the uncouth, obscure sleep — not
once in a blue moon, but at least three hundred and sixty-
five times a year. She ought seriously to think that there is
something uncanny, something mysterious in her ardently
seeking what she ardently dislikes, namely, dull sleep. Some
enquirers do not care so cast a glance — even when reminded
by sages — at their conditions in the sleep state, taking it to
be irrelevant to their questions. They imagine themselves
well-established in a solid world of truth, and there can be
no sense in taking them out of it into a world of shadows
and mist. But the fact remains that the comparison and
coordination of all the three states are most essential for the

full understanding of the true nature of *jagrat*. Again the questioner fancies sleep to be useful for the "relaxation of the body". Relaxation implies an antecedent feeling of tension. We have on many occasions proved the body to be insentient. That being the case how can an insentient object feel a tension? Moreover, if relaxation of the body is the objective, where is the earthly reason of dropping the body completely in this world in bed and going to another world for it? Why cannot it be done right here, where so many other machines are given rest?

The fact is, that what impels us to seek sleep is the longing for the rest and delight of the inner "home", where we gather ourselves, so to say, from the exhausting dissipations caused by the senses, whose "interesting" creation is fictitious, and "beauty" an ephemeral mirage. What we take to be waking is actually dreaming, and our sleep is actually waking into the sanity of dreamlessness. What is darkness for the ignorant is light for the wise, Bhagavan's quotation reads, and its significance we have to study carefully.

Bhagavan explains:

20. "The sleep, dream and waking states are mere phenomena appearing on the Self, which is itself stationary as simple awareness. The same person sleeps, dreams and wakes up. The waking state is perceived to be full of beautiful and interesting things, the absence of which makes one think that sleep is dull. Because you identify yourself with the body you see the world around you and say that the waking state is filled with beautiful things. Sleep appears dull because you are not there as an individual and therefore these things are not perceived. But what is the fact? There is the continuity of Being in all the three states, but not of the individual and the objects.

That which is continuous endures; that which is discontinuous is transitory. Therefore the state of Being is permanent, whereas the body and the world are not." 609

*Note*: This is extremely lucid. It all amounts to saying that because the body which sees "the beautiful and interesting things" in the waking state is absent in sleep, that these things are then also absent. Therefore the world and the body rise and sink together without affecting the being who wakes, dreams and sleeps. Thus the body is not the being, but only the instrument it has chosen for itself to enjoy the beautiful and interesting things, just as one chooses a telescope to see an object ten miles away, which otherwise would remain invisible. The body is no more oneself than the telescope is. Further, the body can be discarded, whereas the being is continuous. Thus the being is the reality, whereas the temporary body is not.

21. "The mind is like *akasa* (ether of space). Just as there are objects in space, so there are thoughts in the mind.... One cannot hope to measure the universe and study the phenomena. It is impossible. For the objects are mental creation; it is like trying to stamp with one's foot on the head of one's shadow; the farther one moves the farther goes the shadow's head." 485

*Note*: We have already seen that space is the mind's extension, containing thoughts which appear to be the external objects. Since the objects are our own creation, pursuing them in the attempt to reach their end is like trying to place one's foot on the head of one's own shadow, which recedes as the body moves nearer, for the more we think the larger will the universe grow, however unwieldy and of incomprehensible immensity it already is.

Therefore the study of the phenomena will lead absolutely nowhere but to the never-ending phenomena — never to the Real which underlies them. All sciences — mathematics, physics, medicine — pertain to the phenomena, the world of space, of time, of experience, of bodies, of action, and perish with them.

> 22. "Are thoughts mere matter?"
> Bhagavan: "Do you mean matter like the things you see around you? But who is the thinker? You admit that he is Spirit. Do you mean that Spirit generates matter? Can Consciousness generate non-consciousness, or light darkness?"                                613

*Note*: The questioner rightly demands clarification of the oft-repeated assertion that the world is merely our thoughts. Bhagavan's answer implies that by "our thoughts" is meant a mere appearance, which has nothing real in it, like the appearance of water in a mirage, which is no water at all.

Thoughts are after all mere vibrations in consciousness, in themselves they are NOTHING, but in our minds they assume ideas or notions of objects — mountains, lands, seas, forests, and the thousands of the things that surround us, — or else how can Brahman or God, who is pure Spirit, generate stones, fire, water, however much the religions of the world may hail Him as their creator? Further, it is utterly inconceivable that He, Who is immaculate radiance as supreme Bliss-Intelligence, should give rise to the abnormal darkness of *avidya*, or to fear, hatred, envy, pain, diseases, etc. The inference is neither world nor *avidya* exists. They are pure fantasy — Consciousness alone is.

Vasishta tells Rama: "The visible world, O Rama, myself, thyself and all things are NOTHING; they are uncreated, unborn; the Supreme Spirit alone exists by Itself.

"As pearls in the sky the world is nonexistent; it is as unreal as the (individual) soul in the void of consciousness."

*(Yoga Vasishta,* III, xiv-xv)

*Yoga Vasishta's* quoted verse clinches the content of the chapter, which has again and again proved that the world is nothing but a state of the mind, that is, a temporary appearance in the mind of its experiencer. By itself it does not exist at all.

It is an oft-repeated truth that the Reality — Self or Brahman — is changeless and ever present — not once present and once absent. The Reality is the experiencer of the states himself. He is present in the *waking,* dreaming, dreamless sleep and *Turiya* (the fourth) or *samadhi,* whereas the world is present only in the waking *(jagrat)* and completely absent in the others. The world with all its mountains, oceans, mighty rivers and mightier volcanos is simply wiped off the slate of the seer's consciousness the moment he steps out of the waking into another state. This proves that the senses which are active only in the waking to make it are the creators of the world. The physical body through the sensory organs — eyes, ears, nose, etc., — which are lodged in it feeds the senses on the impressions received by them from an apparent outside. In no other body this machinery of sense and sense organs are found, which is why its deluding power — *Maya* — prevails only in the waking state *(jagrat)* and why deliverance from it *(Maya)* is sought in *jagrat* only, through the practice of *tapas* — meditation and study. This is the only *maya* known to us — Advaitins — put in the simplest language to unbaffle the baffled seekers and students who love simplicity and direct approach.

## CHAPTER SEVEN

# GOD

1. "Is it possible to have a vision of God?" Bhagavan answers: "Yes, certainly; you see this and that — why not also God? All are always seeing God, but they do not know it. Find out what God is; people see, yet see not, because they know not God."  31

*Note*: That's just it: "They have eyes but do not see, ears but do not hear, noses but do not smell," sings the Psalmist in another context. Because God cannot be seen, tasted, smelt, heard or touched — the only means by which men cognise an object — He, though always present, is not cognised. And if we do not know what God is, what shape, colour or size is He to assume in our vision to convince us that He is God? It poses a terrible dilemma to God when a devotee, who does not have an anthropomorphic pet God of his own, appeals to Him to show His true Self, for whatever shape He would assume the devotee would not be convinced. Moreover, it would certainly not be that of God, Who is formless.

We have previously seen that the world appears to the *Jnani* as Divine, and some teachers go so far as to preach it loudly, thinking they would thereby please their listeners. But the louder they preach it, the less the thoughtful listener is convinced. The latter would argue: If the world is God, then why are we so starved after the vision of God, as the present questioner shows himself to be. If the world is God, there would be complete satisfaction — *Ananda*, Elysium, heavenly joy — everywhere. It is only because the world is not God that we hanker after God, so that we may have peace from the ungodly world. The scriptures are more rational in that they equate the world with the not-self (*Neti-Neti*), with the *gunas*, with the disturbed equilibrium in our consciousness. It is therefore for the *ajnani* (unrealised) the other way round: the world is not only not God, but the reverse of God, so that to go Godward, we have to turn our backs on the world.

Thus he who pins his faith to the five senses can never expect to have the vision of God as God is in Himself, but only as a spurious entity which plays the role of God. It will be an imitation, a symbolic representation of the God the worshipper has in mind or understands best. A Krishna worshipper sees Him as Baby Krishna, a Rama devotee sees Him as Rama, a Christian sees Him as one of the Christian Saints, but the true devotee knows that God has no form of any kind, He being the seer of all sights, hearer of all sounds, smeller of all smells, knower of all knowledge, and thus ever present in a world which consists of nothing but sights, sounds, smells, etc. Bhagavan asks us to know Him thus, when we can say that we have truly known God. This is the highest and only true vision of God.

2.   "Does not Advaita aim at becoming one with God?"
     Bhagavan: "Where is becoming one with God? The thinker is himself ever the Real, a fact which he ultimately realises."                                                    31

*Note: Bhagavan* here, as always, definitely eliminates the distinction between the individual and God, supporting the Srutis by experience. Becoming implies the present non-Being, which is absurd. Being means eternal existence, which is God or eternal truth. And as we admit only one existence, namely, our own, of which alone we are irrefutably sure, it follows that we *are* Being — we *are* now and for ever God Himself or Itself. Advaitins like us are not rattled by dualists who consider the identification of man with God heretical. These have not the foggiest notion of what God is, but make Him in their own image and worship Him as a personality owning, both human weaknesses — partiality, jealousy, injustice, cruelty, petty-mindedness, callousness, and what not — as well as omnipotence. And because their senses are all out, they can understand nothing which is not in terms of solid and liquid, of eyes, ears and noses, and of their peculiar communal beliefs and customs. In the last note we have discussed what in Advaita we mean by God, and if the questioner gets used to that view, Bhagavan's answer will be clear to him.

3.   "Do we not see God in concrete form? "The Master: "Yes, God is seen in the mind. The form and appearance of God-manifestation are determined by the mind of the devotee. But it is not the finality. There is the sense of duality. It is like a dream-vision. After God is perceived, *vichara* commences. That ends in the Realisation of the Self. *Vichara* is the ultimate path. Of course a few find *vichara* practicable. Others find *bhakti* easier."      251

*Note*: This amplifies the first text of this chapter and bears out the reflections thereon, namely, that the sense-bound person sees visions of Gods and saints as forms — the forms in which he expects them to be, or comprehends them best, for God is pure spirit, pure consciousness, which can be apprehended by the pure light of our personal consciousness, because it is the one and the same consciousness which underlies and witnesses all the appearances. Bhagavan is very explicit on this point, namely, "the form and appearance of

God's manifestation are determined by the mind of the devotee, but it is not the finality," because it is the *sankalpa* of the devotee which manifests the duality of the worshipper and the worshipped. Therefore this external form has to be transcended through the internal *vichara*, which will reveal the individual consciousness to be identically the same as the pure Consciousness we call Brahman or absolute Self. For if they were not one and the same Consciousness, the attainment of the latter by the former would be impossible, entirely out of the question.

4.  "How is all-immanent God said to reside in the Ether of the Heart?"
    Bhagavan: "Do we not reside in one place? Do you not say that you are in your body? Similarly God is said to reside in the Heart-lotus. The Heart-lotus is not a place. Some place is mentioned as the place of God, because we think we are in the body. This kind of teaching is meant for those who can appreciate only relative knowledge. Being immanent everywhere, there is no particular place for God. The instruction means 'look within'." 269

*Note*: That the Almighty God, who is infinite and boundless, can squeeze Himself in such a small and uncomfortable hole as the human heart, poses a tremendous problem to the sense-bound person. Bhagavan explains that the heart-lotus is not a physical place, but an apt simile made for the sake of those who "appreciate only relative knowledge", that is, sensuous experience. But the designation of Heart for God is not without foundation: the experience of absolute Being is felt in *samadhi* as pure consciousness in one's inmost being, rather, to be precise, *in the heart of one's being*, because it is blissful as well as being. We are all agreed that joy or any emotion is only felt in the heart — not the muscular heart, but somewhere in our being, which we locate in the chest, though not in the flesh and ribs of the chest. It is in this heart, this subtle emotional centre, that the bliss of the pure consciousness — or God is felt in *samadhi*. This is the meaning of the saying that God is bliss and resides in the ether of the heart. If the whole universe resides in this consciousness, it follows that consciousness pervades the universe. God is thus immanent and resides in the Heart as well. And if you wish to verify it, Bhagavan exhorts you to "look within".

CHAPTER EIGHT

# SCRIPTURES AND SCHOLARSHIP

1.  "The Vedas give conflicting accounts of Cosmogony. Do
    not these impair the credibility of the Vedas?"
    Bhagavan: "The essential aim of the Vedas is to teach us
    the nature of the imperishable *Atman* and show us that
    we are That. As you are satisfied with this aim and
    teaching you should treat the rest as *Arthavada*, auxiliary
    expositions, made for the ignorant who seek to trace
    the genesis of things."                                      30

*Note*: Human society stands at different psychical levels, each
of which requires instructions comprehensible to itself. The
Vedas give these instructions, but reserve their best to the
seeker of the Highest, to whom they reveal the science of
Brahman, the absolute Self. This science alone should
concern us, because it is the science of our own being, of the
eternal Truth. Bhagavan advises us to desist from indulging
in extraneous matters, such as the stories of Creation,
Dissolution, etc. Such stories in the Vedas speak to the fiction
and speculation lovers.

2.  "The Scriptures are useful to indicate the existence of
    the Higher Power (the Self), and the way to gain it.
    Their essence is that much only. When that is assimilated
    the rest is useless. We read so much. Do we remember
    all we read? The essential soaks in the mind and the rest
    is forgotten. So it is with the Sastras."                   62

*Note*: By mentioning memory Bhagavan draws attention to the behaviour of our consciousness in automatically sifting in its highly organised machinery the grain from the chaff, the essential from the unessential, throwing the latter into the limbo, much as a student does when he endeavours to retain the most important parts of his studies, and allows the rest to fall through the sieve of his memory. We have to do the same with regard to what we read in the Scriptures. We must choose what has a direct bearing on the eternal Truth and completely wink at the rest. Judicious study of the Srutis bears the greatest fruit, and this is done only through the guidance of a Master, who is the very embodiment of the Srutis and the soul of the Sastras.

3.  "The ultimate Truth is so simple. It is nothing more than being in the pristine state. That is all that need be said.
    "But people will not be content with simplicity; they want complexity. Because they want something elaborate, attractive and puzzling, so many religions have come into existence. Each of them is so complex and each creed in each religion has its own adherents and antagonists.
    "For example, an ordinary Christian will not be satisfied unless he is told that God is somewhere in the far-off Heavens, not to be reached by us unaided. Christ alone knew Him and Christ alone can guide us. Worship Christ and be saved. If told the simple truth — 'The Kingdom of Heaven is within you' — he is not satisfied and will read complex and far-fetched meanings in such statements. Mature mind alone can grasp the simple truth in all its nakedness."    96

*Note*: Bhagavan is very frank in this text. Not that he wants to attack the established religions, or single out any one of them as the most superstitious and irrational; but, as the teacher of the Absolute, he has to be consistent when appeals are made to his views on the variety of movements that go about in the name of God, the "wisdom" of God, the "truth" of God, and what not, although he is always guarded in his answers, in order not to give offence to the hypersensitive, who is apt to catch fire at the least mention of his religion or "spiritual" institution.

The part that religion should play in the life of an individual, Bhagavan opines, should merely be to show him the truth about himself; not to entertain him with glamorous cosmogony and cosmology, or to frighten him with superstitious inventions, which do more harm than good to his approach to the reality. Bhagavan does not ignore either the ethical side of religion or the well-known fact that not all men are prepared for the Highest Truth. But when the questioner is a seeker of the Highest, he has to be shown nothing less than the Highest, before which an ethical teaching appears as pale as moonlight at midday.

The complexity of which Bhagavan speaks is, no doubt, very strangling, because it obscures the Real; yet there are millions, laymen as well as clergymen, who are always ready to shed the last drop of their blood to defend every syllable of it. Is this complexity — superstitions, accretions, irrelevancies — useful to them? It looks as if it is, at their own level, till they outgrow it. The *adhikari* immediately lays his fingers on it, refutes it outright, and opens himself to the healthy teachings of the Path of the Supreme. The lesser *adhikaris*, although they free themselves from many superstitions, get caught by the "elaborate, attractive and puzzling" — probably *siddhis*, — because they have not yet completely transcended the lower *gunas*, and thus spend a lifetime of wasted efforts. To the Master, Truth is as self-evident as the look of "a gooseberry in the palm of one's hand", for it is nothing but one's "pristine nature", to which the *sadhaka* drives direct and which he eventually never fails to attain.

4.    "The author of *Vritti Prabhakara* claims to have studied 350,000 books before writing this book. *Vichara Sagara* is full of logic and technical terms. But what is the use? Can these ponderous volumes serve any real purpose? Can they give Realisation of the Self? Yet there are people who read them and then seek sages for the sole purpose of seeing if these can meet their questions. To read these volumes, to discover new doubts and to solve them is a source of delight to them. Knowing this to be sheer waste of time, the sages do not encourage such people. Encourage them once and there will be no end.

"Only the Enquiry into the Self can be of use.

"Those familiar with logic and with large books like *Vritti Prabhakara*, *Vichara Sagara* and *Sutra Bhashya* cannot relish small works like *Truth Revealed*, dealing only with the Self and pointedly too; because they have accumulated *vasanas*. Only those whose minds are less muddy, and are pure, can relish small but purposeful works."

332

*Note*: Ponderous are the books scholars read, and even more ponderous the scholars feel themselves to be. They accumulate *vasanas*, the peculiar scholastic *vasanas*, which inflate as they grow, with which sometimes they pester even sages. "Knowing this to be sheer waste of time, the sages do not encourage such people" is, no doubt, autobiographical.

This teaches us the futility of the established logic or of the tiresomely voluminous pseudo spiritual books to guide us on the practical path to the Absolute. Ponderous tomes leave their marks on the mind, and too many marks are bound to conflict with and blur the vision of the Real. What is more, being biased by the massiveness of their "scientific" approach, the scholars become incapable of appreciating the modest, though the best and most pointed approach to truth, when they meet it. They do not even condescend to give it a glance — it is too simple and couched in too few words, and too feebly analytical to be worthy of their consideration. They drop it like hot cake. *"Truth Revealed"* is the translation of a booklet written by Bhagavan himself, consisting of only forty verses, and deal exclusively with the Truth and the way to it, in the simplest style possible. It contains the whole teaching of Advaita philosophy in a nutshell. Some of these scholars sniff at it, because it contains neither critical arguments nor pompous quotations and phraseology and is certainly very poor in bulk.

Bhagavan warns us against the lures and traps of scholarship. What is the use, he asks? Does it bring in Self-realisation? Certainly it does not, and *cannot.* This warning is especially timely in this age which is so excessively prolific in philosophical production with its great appeal to the modern mind.

5.   *"Divya chakshush* (eye sight) is necessary to see the glory of God. Can we not see the glory as the splendour of a million suns?"
Bhagavan: "Oh I see: you want to see the splendour of a million suns. Can you see even that of one sun? Divine light means self-luminosity, self-knowledge. Otherwise who is to bestow a divine eye, and who is to see? Again people read in books that 'hearing, reflection and one-pointedness' are necessary. They think that they must pass through *savikalpa* and *nirvikalpa samadhi* before attaining Realisation. Hence all these questions. Why should they wander in that maze? What do they gain in the end? Only cessation of the trouble of seeking. They will find that the Self is eternal and self-evident. Then why not get repose in the Self even this moment?

"The simple man is satisfied with *japa* or with worship, but the trouble is for the bookworms. Well, well, they also will get on."                                          336

*Note*: The first line shatters the description in books of the Supreme Consciousness as blazing light, or a visual splendour comparable to a million suns. This is an utterly misleading description; for it is nothing of the kind. The light of the Self is the pure knowledge with which we cognise everything, including the Self itself, which in no way stands comparison with any physical radiance. Speaking of divine visions does not mean a special physical or spiritual eye, or the eye of the "clairvoyant", with which someone endows us. According to Bhagavan "Divine sight means self-luminosity", self-knowledge, "the eye of wisdom," or *jnana*; for the Self alone is divine and nothing else. It is called radiant because it is vividly experienced in *samadhi*, free from the obscuring clouds of thoughts and emotions. It is self-luminous because it is self-evident, that is, it knows itself and does not depend on an external knowledge to be known — itself being pure knowledge.

Bhagavan brushes aside book-knowledge as of no use for Self-realisation on special grounds. We learn all the details about the stages on the path from books, or even from the Guru himself, in the hope that by following them we may in the end rest from the stress and strain of a long quest. Bhagavan says, strictly speaking, all this is unnecessary, because the rest we seek is, like the goal itself, even now available to us. We have, if we are alert enough, only to open the eye of our intuition to perceive it; for it is our very self, the very seeker himself, from which at no time he is separated. Books will be useful only if the seeker is unable to perceive himself by himself. Cases are known of very unsophisticated seekers who have scarcely ever read a book in their life and who have nevertheless reached the goal quickly by merely adhering to their peculiar form of *sadhana*. There are, on the other hand, thousands who have read books without number and who have not, for that reason, advanced an inch spiritually.

As for the books themselves, Bhagavan does not criticise them indiscriminately; for he himself has written some, and has the highest respect for some famous works and their great Acharya authors. Besides, study and reflections sharpen and polish the intellect and are thus very essential in this *marga*. What he criticises are those works, which, while professing to teach truth, do not retain its purity throughout, and sometimes mislead by false comparisons, exaggerations and useless arguments, as we have seen him doing in the previous texts. The books of the "bookworms", namely, of the wrangling and brain-racking argumentative type, are utterly useless for the purpose of the Supreme Quest. Yet in the end Bhagavan holds a hope even for the "bookworms" — "Well, well, they also will get on."

CHAPTER NINE

# THE SELF OR REALITY

1.    "The habits of the mind (*vasanas*) hinder the realisation
      of the Self, and in order to overcome the *vasanas* we
      have to realise the Self. Is this not a vicious circle?"
      The Master: "It is the ego which raises these difficulties
      and then complains of an apparent paradox. Find out
      who is making the enquiries and the Self will be found.
      "The Self is ever present; there exists nothing without it.
      It is the witness of the three states: the sleep, dream and
      waking, which belong to the ego. The Self transcends the
      ego. Did you not exist even in sleep? It is only in the
      waking state that you describe the experience of sleep as
      being unawareness: therefore the consciousness when
      asleep is the same as that when awake. If you know what
      this waking consciousness is, you will know the con-
      sciousness which witnesses all the three states. Such
      consciousness could be found by seeking the consciousness
      as it was in sleep."                                    13

*Note*: The questioner sees an undoubted vicious circle in
the preceding answers (not mentioned here) of the Master,
which Bhagavan solves by asking him to enquire into the
seer of the vicious circle, namely, himself. Why does he want
to realise the Self, that is, his own self? Because he pleads
ignorance of it, yet at the same time he is fully aware of it as
the questioner himself. Is not that a paradox? The self he
knows, or imagines he knows, is the same self he seeks, or
else he would be two instead of only one. How can he get
out of this dilemma?

That everyone is sure of his own reality as intelligence is proved by his statements: "I know," "I study," "I smell," "I think," "I decide," etc., but the confusion begins the moment he gives a distinctive name to himself — Peter — as a body, different from all other bodies.

Therefore the "vicious circle" is due to the wrong mental attitude of the questioner about his own identity, and to dissipate this Bhagavan adds the other explanations, the substance of which is something like this:

The Self is pure awareness or knowledge. And, because it is pure knowledge, it has to be present in every experience as its knower, or else how can a thing or state be known? This knower we call Self. So the Self is the knower of all things and all states. It must be present in the waking, dreaming and deep sleep states, which "belong to the ego", that is, which every individual or ego — Peter — experiences. Therefore the ego is the Self itself. But, because the Self is one and indivisible, being pure consciousness, and the ego is known by names, such as Peter or John, and by form — the form of Peter or of John — that we say that the Self transcends the ego, that is, being without names and forms. Names and forms are thus the cause of the illusion of a difference between the two, because they make the one consciousness to appear many.

Now the *sadhaka* arrives at the knowledge of his being nameless and formless, one in all names and forms — in all beings — by arguing his positions, as Bhagavan does in this text, in every one of these three states and relates them to each other. In *jagrat*, for example, I am aware of all the *jagrat* things that surround me, including my own self as Peter, and my body, or form, which measures so much by so much. Then I go to the dream state, where I am neither Peter, nor have his form, but somebody else, say, X, with the form of X. Then I pass on to the dreamless state, where I am aware of nothing, of neither name nor form, neither Peter nor X.

Reviewing in *jagrat* the whole of this process, I sum it up thus: I, the conscious knower, assume the name and form of Peter in *jagrat*, of X in *svapna*, but remain nameless and formless, as my pure self, in *sushupti*. Therefore Peter and X, are not I. Similarly the gross body of the former and the subtle body of the latter are not essential to me, but superimposed on me when I witness the first two states. With the removal of the restrictions of names and forms from myself, I remain the same being alone, free from all limitations and qualities. This aloneness is known as *kaivalya*. And to experience it in *jagrat* we have to take to *sadhana*, which removes the obstructions and enables the 'I' to perceive itself as the pure, eternal Self. This *sadhana* and this knowledge of the Real are the main purpose of the Vedas. The state of *kaivalya* for the embodied obtains only in *sushupti* and *samadhi*, unconsciously in the former but consciously in the latter.

2.     "How to know the real 'I' as distinct from the false 'I'?" The Master answered: "Is there anyone who is not aware of himself? Each one knows yet does not know the Self. A strange paradox."                    43

*Note*: In the last note we amply dealt with this "strange paradox", and showed that there is no such thing as "false 'I'," but only false notions about the 'I' which mistakes its *upadhis* or qualities, its names and forms for itself. Because of this transposition of the 'I' from its being the seer to being the seen, that is, the name and form of Peter — to continue the idea of the last note — that the grave error of its being false, vulnerable and mortal is committed. Hence the desire to search for the real and deathless 'I' arises.

3. "Unbroken 'I' 'I' is the boundless Ocean; the 'I'-thought is a bubble on it and is called *jiva* or individual. The bubble too is water. When it bursts, it mixes with the ocean. When it remains a bubble it is still part of the ocean." 92

*Note*: Bhagavan gives a practical illustration. The 'I' 'I' is the pure, nameless and formless being: it is the ocean of consciousness. The bubble (or 'I'-thought) is naught but water in substance, that is, also consciousness, but in form, that is, in its understanding of itself it has a separate individuality — ego or *jiva*, the mortal and ignorant Peter, or Ramaswamy. This false view persists so long as the *jiva* does not perceive itself nameless and formless in *jagrat*, as it stands in *sushupti*. But the moment it does the bubble bursts; the false appearance of separateness immediately dissolves, and the *jiva* cognises itself as 'I', the ocean of the 'I' consciousness. All that has happened is not the transform-ation of the *jiva* into the Supreme Consciousness, but the correction of its notion of itself as *jiva*, as a bubble entirely separate from other bubbles and from the Ocean, whereas in fact it has at no time been other than the Ocean of Consciousness.

4. "The Self is only one. If limited it is the ego. If unlimited it is infinite and is the Reality. The bubbles are different from one another and numerous, but the ocean is only one. Similarly the egos are many, whereas the Self is one and only one. When told that you are not the ego, realise the Reality, why do you still identify yourself with the ego?" 146

*Note*: The beginning of this text is not properly formulated. The "If" is troublesome, as most "ifs" are. What it means is this: the Self is always unlimited, and, because unlimited, it cannot but be an indivisible whole. Now what happens is, as it has been said above, that though the individual is the unlimited Self, he feels himself limited. To this feeling of limitedness he owes his separate individuality. In other words, ego is the Self who is under the illusion of being limited and disappears when the feeling of limitedness disappears, which Bhagavan clarifies in the end when he finds fault with the questioner that despite repeated assurances to the contrary, the latter continues to feel himself the limited ego.

As for the analogy of the bubble and the ocean, it has been amply dealt with in the last note. One thing more need be said about it here, namely, like all analogies it suffers from the drawback of inadequacy, in that the bubbles in the ocean are insentient, material bubbles (see next note), whereas the *jivas* are imaginary, mere conceptions of limitedness. That is why Bhagavan always reminds us that "if you search for the ego, it will disappear", its being an illusory conception.

5.    "Destroy the ego by seeking its identity (with the Self). Because the ego is not an entity it will automatically vanish and Reality will shine forth by itself. This is the direct method."                                   146

6.    "In *Yoga Vasishta* it is said, 'What is real is hidden from us, but what is false is revealed as true.' We are all along experiencing the Reality, still we do not know it. Is this not a wonder?"                                    146

*Note*: This is very interesting in that it definitely declares the world to be false. Whatever is seen, thought or imagined is an illusion — a mere appearance; for the reality can never be perceived or conceived. Even the *jivas*, which are said to be real, are not perceived and do not actually see one another as knowers, as consciousness. What we see of each other are only the insentient, objective parts of us, that is, the *upadhis:*

height, breadth, colour, smell, sound, mental abilities, expressed thoughts or action, etc., but never the mind itself, their container. In other words, we see the outer coats of one another, and never the Self which they conceal and which is common to all. This is the meaning of the above quotation from *Yoga Vasishta:* what we perceive does not exist, and what exists always we cannot perceive.

To take an example, Mr. Paul is an actor in a play. Once he plays the role of a judge, once of a lover, once of a dacoit, and once he acts as a big bear or a chimpanzee. All these entities are unreal, mere impersonations of Mr. Paul, yet they alone we perceive on the stage and not their substratum Mr. Paul, notwithstanding his being the only real presence. Similarly, though the Reality is ever present as the seer and actor of all phenomena, like Mr. Paul on the stage, we perceive only that which does not exist, namely, the phenomena — the chimpanzee, the bear, etc. The world no more exists than the chimpanzee and the dacoit exist on the stage. This seeing what does not exist and remaining blind to what really exists is the case of every person in the world and is the cause of all his misfortunes. Our science calls it *Maya*. Bhagavan puts it mildly when he exclaims, "Isn't that a wonder?" It is an unconscious mass blindness indeed, a mass hypnosis not to see Mr. Paul who stands all the while before our eyes, but we swear to the reality of the bear and the dacoit who are not there at all.

7.  "There is only one consciousness, but we speak of several kinds of consciousnesses — body-consciousness, self-consciousness, etc. These are only relative states of the same absolute consciousness. Without consciousness time and space do not exist. They appear in consciousness. It is like a screen on which these are cast as pictures, and move as in a cinema show. The absolute consciousness is

our real nature. Everyone's experience proves the existence of only one consciousness."                     199

*Note*: Consciousness is "one only" and changeless. It cannot be otherwise. Turn it however we may, the notion of a variety of consciousnesses we meet with in certain schools of thought and in psychology proves untenable and defeats itself, being based on the ignorance of the nature and functions of consciousness. Being incognisable except in Yoga there is all this confused thinking about it. Consciousness or pure mind is the formless intelligence through which we perceive all things. Ideas, notions, sensations, perceptions, are representations in the consciousness, BUT NOT THE CONSCIOUSNESS ITSELF. They are in ceaseless flux; whereas the consciousness that is aware of them is fixed, or else it would not be aware of their change. It is constant, for it has no qualities whatsoever to divide, multiply, or change it. Thus body-consciousness simply means awareness of the body and its behaviour, like the awareness of any other representation made to it. Awareness is like the clean mirror which reflects all the objects that are presented before it. What is known as states of consciousness does not qualify the consciousness, which has no other state but its own. The states are mere appearances in the consciousness, that is, in the subject who witnesses them. Bhagavan compares consciousness to the screen on which pictures are projected. It is the pictures that change, and not the screen. It is the acting of the aforesaid Mr. Paul and his impersonations on the stage that change, and not Mr. Paul, who is constant and can act an infinite number of parts without himself changing. Time and space are, like other ideas and notions, objects of the Consciousness outside of which they have no existence.

8.   "A madman clings to his *samskaras*, whereas a *Jnani* does
     not. This is the only difference between the two. A man
     running the course of his *samskaras*, when taught that
     he is the Self, the teaching affects his mind, and his
     imagination runs riot. His experiences are only according
     to his imagination of the state of the Self.
     "When a man is ripe to receive the instructions and his
     mind is about to sink into the Heart, the instructions work
     in a flash and he realises the Self all right. In others there
     is always a struggle."                                       275

*Note*: The context of this text is the case of a young man,
who, when once was looking at the picture of Bhagavan in
his own house, saw the picture move, which frightened him
considerably. The fear continued even after he came to
Tiruvannamalai and saw Bhagavan in person. As long as he
was in the presence of the Master, he had no fear, but the
moment he remained alone the fear returned.

   This is one of the varieties of experience which some
people who come to the Ashram, or worship Bhagavan even
from a distance without understanding him, undergo, because
they rely more on their imagination of Bhagavan rather than
on what he in reality is or stands for. Bhagavan's answer is a
warning against the tricks of their imagination. I once
witnessed a case which appeared tragic in the beginning, but
ended humorously. The humour did not become apparent
till very recently, after twenty years. But not all cases have a
humorous denouement. Some are very tragic, indeed, in that
they affect permanently the mind, as, for example, the fatal
case of the young man recorded in pp. 314-15 of the *Talks*.
Others are tragicomedies, victims of which are both the sexes.
The comedies fall largely to the share of the fair sex, because
the "riot" of their imagination runs gentler than with their
masculine counterparts, and move in the familiar grooves of
*saris*, colour of dress, invasion of her heart and mind by the

spirit of Bhagavan, or even petty conversations with Ishwara — God the Creator — Whom Bhagavan "sends" her, and so on. But the hallucinations of men are much more serious. At least in one or two cases they led to the disruption of the family life. That is why the seer of visions and supersensuous phenomena is constantly reminded to be on his guard. To aspire for the Highest, one has to develop a strong common sense and a solidly practical mind.

The ripe man, Bhagavan tells us, forms a more or less clear notion of the Self when he hears of it, so that he is steady enough to know the direction his *sadhana* should take and applies himself well, not allowing his imagination to have the better of him. The others have much an uphill work to do before they become ripe. Even to understand the teaching itself much effort will be necessary. This is their struggle, the labour-pangs of their salvation.

9.   "It is said that the Guru can make his disciple realise the Self by transferring some of his own power to him: is this true?"
     Bhagavan: "Yes, the Guru does not bring about Self-realisation, but simply removes the obstacles to it. The Self is always realised. So long as you seek Self-realisation the Guru is necessary. Guru is the Self. Take the Guru to be the real Self and yourself the individual. The disappearance of this sense of duality is removal of ignorance. So long as duality persists in you the Guru is necessary. Because you identify yourself with the body, you imagine the Guru to be the body. You are not the body, nor is the Guru. You are the Self and so is he. This knowledge is gained by what you call Self-realisation."
                                                            282

*Note*: It will be noticed that the question has not been given a direct answer; for Bhagavan is very often reluctant to give a direct contradiction to the statement, or the alleged statement, of a well-known saint, but the contradiction is implied in the answer. Bhagavan does not recognise the possibility of transmitting a power to a person to make him realise the Self. In fact no such power is at all necessary. What is necessary for the cognition of the Real is not an addition but a subtraction — the removal of the sense of duality which covers the One consciousness. This consciousness is the seeker's own self, which is always present: it does not lie within the power of the personal Guru to confer or withhold. It is there all the time, and if the disciple does not perceive it, it is because he mistakes his body for it; and, as he fails to perceive himself as a thinker, he fails also to see the Guru as a thinker but as a mere body, thus establishing a duality: himself as different from the Guru. All the Guru can do is to help him correct this false identification, so that the disciple may eventually perceive himself in his true essence, as intelligence rather than as a pile of flesh.

Then the questioner turns to ask about the necessity or otherwise of the Guru, and the Master confirms the necessity, so long as this false identification and the view of duality rule the day with the seeker, who is taken to be always in duality till he realises the non-duality, which is his Illumination or *jnana*.

10. "Look how every person believes in his own existence. Does he look in the mirror to see his being? His awareness of his existence gives him the assurance of it. But he compares it with the body, etc. Why should he do that? Is he aware of his body in sleep? He is not, yet he does not cease to exist while in sleep. He has therefore only to be aware of his being and this will be evident to him."

363

*Note*: This is extremely lucid. Paraphrasing it, it means this: no one need look in the mirror to know that he exists; for this knowledge is already available to him. We are aware of our existence with a certainty which is unshakeable. Therefore the certainty of our being is the one element in us which can never be lost. We may doubt all other things, but this one *never*. Even in deep sleep we exist as we admit it later in *jagrat*. This is not an intuited knowledge, nor a reported knowledge, nor an inferred knowledge, but a direct, immediate knowledge. So long as we hold on to this pure knowledge of our existence, to this awareness of our being, there can be no difficulty, no ignorance for us whatsoever. *But the trouble is that we do not*: the moment we see the body, we immediately rush at it, hug it and call it 'I'. This is our fall: this is the genesis of our disturbed peace. So long as we do not see the body, as in dreamless sleep or *samadhi*, we are in supreme peace — we are in our own state, our own naked being. But as soon as we return to *jagrat* and re-enter the body, the body becomes that being, that 'I'. We confer the consciousness of the being on the unconscious body, and then woe betide us!

It can be now seen that when people speak of gaining MUKTI, Bhagavan corrects them that there is nothing to be gained or added by the *sadhana*, meaning that it is not *gaining*, but *returning to the status quo ante*, to the condition which prevailed before the body entered our sphere of perception, to the bodiless being.

11. "How is one to know the Self?" The Master answers: "Knowing the Self is being the Self. You are aware of yourself even though the Self cannot be objectified. It is because you have got accustomed to relative knowledge that you identify yourself with it. Who is to know the Self? Can the body know it?"                                    363

*Note*: This is a continuation of the previous text. Supreme Knowledge and Supreme Being are one and the same. *Chit* is also *Sat*. Awareness of the Being means knowledge of one's own existence, that is, Self-knowledge. Awareness and Being are therefore simultaneous and identical. To say 'I am not aware of myself' is thus logically wrong — a contradiction in terms. Self-awareness is admitted in the confession 'I am'. By "you got accustomed to relative knowledge", is meant that in *jagrat* we are aware of nothing but of objects — *jagrat* is the sphere of objects, though in fact no objects at all exist. *Jagrat* is a mental state, wherein the senses have a free hand to manifest their powers to our consciousness in the form of smells, tastes, sounds, colours, etc., which we assemble in our minds and interpret as objects. We thus lose the being in the perception of imaginary, synthetic objects. The 'I', though aware of its existence, gets confused by its own objectivity, and erroneously projects this awareness on the insentient body, turning it into the sentient Self. This is the true Fall of Man.

12. "Is there a sixth sense to feel 'I AM'?"
    Bhagavan: "Do you deny your existence? Do you not remain yourself even in sleep? As for the senses, they work only periodically. Their works begin and end; whereas the 'I' continues in sleep as well as now. There must be a substratum on which the activities of the senses depend. Where do they appear and merge? There must be a single substratum. That is the Self of which they are not independent. It is the power which works through them."                                    363

*Note*: The questioner, like most beginners, is a bit confused about his 'I AM'. He is perfectly aware of his own existence, but is unable to place his fingers on the 'I' and say 'This am I'. So he enquires whether a sixth sense can do it; for neither the five senses nor the body can cognise the Self. Bhagavan's counter-question, "Do you deny your existence?" implies that even a tenth sense cannot do it, for the senses are *jada* (insentient) and can cognise nothing. The cogniser is the Self alone. A smell, for example, is a smell only to the smeller, without whom it is just nothing. Moreover, the senses are functions of the Self only in *jagrat*. Postulating a sense to know the Self, therefore, is postulating the contained to contain the container.

The Self, therefore, must attempt the knowledge of itself: there only duality finds no accommodation: there only the knower and the known are identically the same 'I AM', the substratum of both.

> 13.    "The individual is sentient and cannot be without consciousness. The Self is pure consciousness. Yet man identifies himself with the body which is insentient and does not say 'I am the body'. Someone else says so. The unlimited Self does not say it either. Who then is saying it? A spurious 'I' which arises between the pure consciousness and the insentient body and which imagines itself limited to the body. Seek this and it will vanish as a phantom. That phantom is the ego or individuality.
> "All the Shastras are written for the purpose of eliminating this phantom. The present state is mere illusion. Our aim should be simply to remove this illusion — to disillusion ourselves."    427

*Note*: In the first four notes of this chapter we made an extensive study of the relation of the ego to the Self and of the fictitious nature of the ego. Here Bhagavan tackles the subject from a different angle.

The body is not sentient and, therefore, unaware of itself to say 'I am this body'. The Self, though it is pure sentience, but, because it is unlimited, it does not limit itself to a body to say 'I am this body' either. If neither pure sentience nor pure insentience can say 'I am this body', here must be a third principle which partakes of the nature of both that can say it. But a principle which is sentient as well as insentient does not exist — it contradicts itself. Therefore such a principle can be only imaginary — "spurious." We call it *ego* or *individuality* to mean sentience gone amuck, thoroughly under the influence of delusion, from which to save it all the Shastras have been written and all Gurus have taken birth.

To sum up: the ego is the Supreme Self itself imagining itself an insentient body. An emphasis must be laid on this psychical error — the imagination element, — which is responsible for the spurious entity, man the ego, that is, man as he imagines himself to be, and *not* as he in reality is. I think this is a very clear picture of the ego, which continues to give trouble till the Self is realised.

14. "You speak of the vision of Siva. Vision is always of an object, which implies the existence of the subject. Whatever appears must also disappear. A vision can never be eternal. But Siva is eternal. He is the consciousness. He is the Self.
"TO BE is to realise — hence I AM THAT I AM. I AM is Siva. Nothing can be without Him. Therefore enquire 'Who am I?' Sink deep and abide as the Self. That is Siva as BE-ing. Do not expect to have visions of Him."

450

*Note*: This is an answer to a European lady who had embraced Hinduism in the Shaiva cult and had been having the blissful vision of Siva off and on since her initiation. Now she desires this vision to be "everlasting". Bhagavan answers that she is asking the impossible: visions can never be everlasting, for in their very nature they are mere appearances, which have no basis in reality. Reality alone is everlasting. Therefore to have the everlasting bliss of Siva is to be Siva Himself. And Siva, being the Supreme Consciousness, is the very self of all seers, all hearers and all knowers, the enquirer herself. Thus to be Siva merely means to be oneself as that Consciousness, stripped of all sights and all thoughts, that is, simply TO BE.

"Nothing can be without Siva" implies that without a seer there can be no sight and, so, no seen. All that is seen therefore must depend upon the percipient consciousness. Consciousness is thus the substratum of all that exists, i.e., present in all experiences.

If Bhagavan mentions Siva as the BE-ing, it is merely in answer to the question of the enquirer. Any other deity can be substituted for Siva without prejudicing the answer, so long as we understand by it the subject, the knower himself. This is confirmed by the next text.

15.   "There is no being who is not conscious and therefore who is not Siva. Not only he is Siva but also all else. Yet he thinks in sheer ignorance that he sees the universe in diverse forms. But if he sees the Self he will not be aware of his separateness from the universe. Siva is then seen as the universe. But (unfortunately) the seer does not see the background. Think of the man who sees only the cloth and not the cotton of which it is made, or the pictures and not the screen; or the letters which he reads and not the paper on which they are written. Siva is both the Being assuming the forms in the universe as well as the consciousness that sees them. That is to say Siva is the background underlying both the subject and the object — Siva in repose and Siva in action. Whatever it is said to be, it is only Consciousness, whether in repose or in action."     450

*Note*: It is now evident that Siva is not other than the seer. The last part of this text which makes the absolute consciousness to be "in repose" as well as "in action" is a good answer to the doctrinaire theory that *Chaitanya* does not include the active senses. If it does not include them, whence then do they arise and enact a world? They answer that the senses do not exist at all — all is *Maya*, which implies that *Maya* is the creator of the senses, which is absurd. The senses are, like memory, space-sense, time-sense, etc., undeniable, for they are responsible for the appearance of an external world, whereas *Maya* is the name given to this appearance, this illusion. *Maya* is thus not the parent but the offspring of the senses. Therefore, the senses are the activity of *Chaitanya*, the Pure Consciousness, but, to repeat, an APPARENT activity, which displays a world that does not exist, like a dream. It is an activity which is within the consciousness, though it appears to be without it, an activity which does not affect the consciousness itself. And, being an appearance within the consciousness, it is the consciousness itself, that is, of the same nature as its substratum; for it cannot be of an alien nature, since there exists nothing but pure consciousness. Thus the world is Siva Himself. He is BEING as well as DOING — Repose as well as Action. And this will not be realised as such until Siva is first realised as BEING, because BEING is His very nature, whereas DOING is only an appearance in Him.

Unless action is understood to be a mere appearance in Being, the true nature of the object will ever remain a puzzle to the student of metaphysics. This is of fundamental importance for the proper apprehension of the relation of the perceptions to their seer, of the changeless Self to the ever-changing phenomena, of the screen, to use Bhagavan's analogy, to the pictures which move on it.

16. "There must be stages of progress for gaining the Absolute. Are there grades of Reality?"
Bhagavan: "There are no grades of Reality. There are grades in the experience of the *jiva*."                    132

*Note*: "Grades of Reality?" Reality is perfect because it is partless, integral, and changeless, or else it contradicts itself. So, Reality is not affected by evolution, nor is it divisible into a number of imperfect beings who need the evolution to attain perfection. We have seen elsewhere that the *jiva* is the Self itself, but deluded. The appearance of multiplicity of *jivas* is an illusion due to the unfoldment of the senses which create qualities and hence differences. Bhagavan says that it is not the Self that has grades but the experiences of the *jivas*. Thus the difference between the savage and the *Jnani* is one of experience, that is, of mental outlooks and not of substance — of being.

17. "There is a multiplicity of *jivas*. *Jivas* are certainly many."
Bhagavan: "*Jiva* is called so because he sees the world. A dreamer sees many *jivas* in dream, but all of them are not real. The dreamer alone exists and he sees all. So it is with the individuals and the world."                    571

*Note*: This is lucid enough to need no comment, except applying it also to the common world, where all men perceive the same objects, same colours, same sounds, same heat or cold, etc. The critics argue that if the world is the senses, as Vedanta says, individual senses would show exclusively individual worlds, so that there would be as many worlds as there are human beings with no connection with one another, which experience disproves. Bhagavan answers that all the senses, all the men and all the worlds are the dreams or thoughts of the *jiva*, which alone exists as the dreamer or thinker. As the *jiva* in dream sees other *jivas* with bodies and senses, without any of them enjoying real existence, so it does in the waking state (*jagrat*). *Jagrat* is called waking only in comparison with the dream state known to us, because the senses are then all out to intensify the illusion of a real external world, whereas the dream state feeds on mere impressions carried over from the state of *jagrat*, and not on the senses, which are then withdrawn.

18. "If the Self is one, when a man is liberated, all men must be also liberated."
Bhagavan: "Ego, world and individuals all appear due to the personal *vasanas:* when these perish, that person's hallucinations also perish.... The fact is that the Self is never bound and thus there can be no release."

571

*Note:* In the last text Bhagavan declares that the multiplicity of *jivas* perceived in the waking state do not, like the dream *jivas*, really exist. Here he adds that they are the *vasanas* of the personal *jiva*. When the *vasanas* perish at Liberation, the hallucination of other *jivas'* existence also perish, so that the question of their Liberation will evidently not arise.

CHAPTER TEN

# HEART AND MIND

1. "That the physical heart is on the left it cannot be denied. But the heart of which I speak is not physical and is only on the right side. It is my experience, no authority is required by me. Still you can find confirmation of it in a Malayali Ayurvedic book and in *Sita Upanishad*."  4

*Note*: This is an authoritative statement on Bhagavan's own experience, which in its practical aspect is of no help to the meditator. The locus of the Heart, whether to the right or to the left, need not worry us (see text 9 below), because when one is in it, that is, in *samadhi*, not only the chest but the body and the whole world disappear. When *dhyana* matures, the Heart automatically reveals itself without any special effort to seek its corresponding place in the physical body.

2. "The *jiva* is said to remain in the Heart in deep sleep, and in the brain in the waking state. Heart is not the muscular cavity which propels blood. It denotes in the Vedas and the scriptures the centre whence the notion 'I' springs. Does it spring from the ball of flesh? It does not, but from somewhere within us, from the centre of our being. The 'I' has no location. Everything is the Self. There is nothing but the Self. So the Heart must be said to be the entire body as well as the universe, conceived as 'I'. But to help the *abhyasi* we have to indicate a definite place in the universe, or the body, for it. So this Heart is pointed out as the seat of the Self.

But in truth we are everywhere; we are all that is, and
there is nothing else." 29

*Note*: Heart therefore has no locus at all. Its other names
are Self, 'I', being, pure mind, etc. It is called Heart due to
its being the source from which the universe rises. In the
last note we observed that in *samadhi* Heart reveals itself as
completely independent of any place. Then why does
Bhagavan locate it in the right chest? He does not locate it in
the flesh and bones of the right chest, but only in
consciousness at the level of that region, much as we locate
the levels of certain objects in space as corresponding to those
of certain parts of our body. Nevertheless, because this
consciousness has direct relations with the body, it must have
a point of contact with it, a switchboard, so to say, in the
subtle counterpart of the body, from which it switches the
body off and on. This switchboard is felt in *samadhi* in the
subtle counterpart of the right chest.

   To the highly critical mind there appears a contradiction
in the statements of Bhagavan, who, on the one hand makes
Heart to be everywhere and nowhere, and on the other fixes
it in the right chest, from which (as in the next text) the
*sushumna nadi* rises, and where the *jiva* retires in sleep, etc.
The apparent contradiction is due to the perception of the
body, which has to be related to the mind, or the intelligent
principle which acts and perceives through it. The mind has
thus to be shown in a dual aspect, the one as the pervader of
the body, and thus hypothetically limited to its shape, and
the other as limitless and free. More of this in the next item.

3.   "Atma is the Heart itself. Its manifestation is in the brain.
     The passage from the Heart to the brain might be
     considered to be through the *sushumna*, or a nerve (*nadi*)
     with some other name. The Upanishads speak of *pare*

*leena*, meaning that the *sushumna* or such *nadis* are all comprised in *Para*, i.e., the *Atma nadi*. The Yogis say that the current rising up to *sahasrara* (brain) ends there. That experience is not complete. For *jnana* they must come to the Heart. *Hridaya* (Heart) is the Alpha and Omega."                                                    57

*Note*: From the Heart the body sprouts. The energy, life and consciousness — the only prime elements of the body and likewise of the universe — stream out of the Heart by the first channel, or *nadi*, straight to the head, from which they run down to all parts of the body through various *nadis*. We need not give names to the *nadis* to avoid conflicts between the locations and names given by one authority and those given by another. Names and forms are the cause of the world illusion, so they are also in metaphysics. Bhagavan simply wishes to indicate these facts about the distribution of life and consciousness to the remotest points in the body through *nadis*, beginning with the *Para nadi*, so that the student may know the function of this *nadi* in the attainment of *jnana*. Because all the *nadis* from the body end in the *sahasrara*, the *Kundalini* yogi, the *Hatha* yogi, and in fact all yogis who practise *pranayama* take the *sahasrara* to be the terminal point of their *sadhana*; whereas the *Dhyana* yogi, also called *Raja* yogi, *Vichara* yogi, etc. adds one more stage for the complete and absolute Emancipation. This last stage runs through the *Para nadi*, also called *Amrita nadi*, because, being of the purest *sattva*, it is extremely blissful and leads straight to the Heart.

   "Its manifestation in the brain" needs some explanation. It is common experience that when people speak of the mind, they always imagine it to be the brain itself, and scientists, who are so sure of themselves, make matters worse when they declare the brain to be the thinker, which is of course wrong, because the brain is as insentient and as incapable of thinking as any other part of the body. If the whole is insentient, so are the parts. This error is due to the manifestation of the *jiva's* activities through the cerebral tissue, which is as it were its telegraph office, which transmits to it all the signals received from the various sense organs and the nervous system, etc. But the home of the *jiva* is the Heart, which is the cosmic storehouse of all the creative impulses. To this home the *jiva* returns with the senses when it retires from the body in sleep, in what is known as "death" and, finally, for good in *mukti*.

4. "The Heart is not physical; it is spiritual *Hridaya* = *hrit* + *ayam*, which means 'that is the Centre'. It is that from which thoughts arise, on which they subsist and where they are resolved. Thoughts are the content of the mind and they shape the universe. The Heart is thus the centre of all. It is said by the Upanishads to be Brahman. Brahman is the Heart." 97

*Note*: This text is the quintessence of the Vedas. Thoughts rise from, subsist in, and dissolve into the Heart: "they shape the universe." This is a pregnant statement. It makes the substance of the universe to be nothing but thoughts, a mere mental vapour. This surpasses even the subjective idealism of the Western philosophers.

"Thoughts are (the products as well as) the content of the mind" is significant, inasmuch as it makes the mind not simply *manas*, as it is usually wrongly translated in Indian metaphysics, but the consciousness which produces, contains, and perceives the thoughts, synonymous with the Heart or Brahman. Bhagavan often equates the pure mind with Brahman, which is as it should be. *Manas* may be rendered as intellect or as a bundle of thoughts and sensations, or perhaps the processes of thought. Sometimes mind is also used in the sense of *manas*. At all events the student will do well to remember this dual meaning of MIND and avoid confusion.

That "the Heart is the centre of All" does not mean that it is not also the circumference. Bhagavan makes it in this text the container of all thoughts, that is, of the universe — centre, circumference, as well as all that comes in between them:

> "Verily as space is boundless, so is the ether within the Heart. Both heaven and earth, fire and air, the sun and the moon, also the lightning and the stars, and whatever is, as well as whatever is not in the universe — all are within this vacuity (Heart)."
>
> (*Chandogya Upanishad*, IX, i. 3)

5.   "How to realise the Heart? There is no one who even for a trice fails to experience the Self. He is the Self. The Self is the Heart. When asked who you are, you place your hand on the right side of the chest and say 'I am', thereby you unknowingly point out the Self. The Self is thus known."                                                           97

*Note*: Here we have a pointer to the locus of the Heart in the body, rather in the subtle ambience of the body. It is instinctive in us to use the right hand rather than the left in pointing to our own person. Why do we not for the purpose place the hand on the head, cheeks, or, say, the spinal chord — or, for the matter of that, the legs or feet — instead of the right chest alone? Unless there is an immediate relation between this part of the chest and the 'I', we would not straightaway and as a matter of course, drive direct to it when we wish to stress our identity. When we want to indicate the mind or the thinking agency we point to the head, but for the 'I' we point to the chest. Isn't that a clear admission of the superiority of the heart over the brain? The Heart is the 'I', the totality of Being, whereas the brain is the seat of its thoughts only.

Pointing exclusively to the chest to indicate one's person has yet another weighty significance. It automatically excludes the other parts of the body from being the 'I', as witness the fact that we resent a reference to the nails, hair, the bodily secretions and excretions, etc., as being our 'I', in fact we instinctively know that even the ribs and flesh of the chest are not the 'I', notwithstanding our demonstrating them as such. We take the body as a whole for 'I', yet in detail we deny it. This anomalous behaviour of our mind in this respect is so glaringly obvious that nothing but wrong habits keep us blind to it. Anomalies multiply as we probe deeper into the relation of the body to the consciousness. That is why *vichara* or enquiry is insisted on in this path to expose the ridiculous inconsistencies of our beliefs and attitudes, so that by correcting them we may attain to the truth of ourselves and of the world around us.

6.   "The Cosmic Mind, being not limited by the ego, has nothing separate from itself and is therefore only aware. This is what the Bible means by 'I am that I Am'."

                                                              187

*Note*: The Cosmic Mind is equated in Advaita and by Bhagavan with Brahman, since it is "only aware". It will be readily observed that this Mind has nothing to do with the Cosmic Mind of the Western mystics, which has its own significance — whatever that may be — different from that of the Advaitic Brahman. Biblical Jehovah is written in Hebrew YHWH, which is derived from the verb HAYA (to be), and means EVER IS, 'I AM THAT I AM,' or BEING, exactly as Advaita means by Brahman or SAT.

7.    "The mind now sees itself diversified as the universe. If the diversity is not manifest, it remains in its own essence, that is, the Heart. The Heart is the only reality. The mind is only a transient phase. To remain as one's Self is to enter the Heart. Entering the Heart means remaining without distractions."                                    252

*Note*: The mind turns into the universe. When it perceives the universe, or diversity, the latter impresses itself on its pure surface, so that its attention is constantly centred on the diversity and not on itself. If the diversity is eliminated, the mind will perceive itself in its essence, its own naked purity. Then it is said to have entered the Heart — in fact it is itself the Heart. This is its undisturbed state, the reposeful state of *samadhi*.

The covering of the mind by thoughts is evidently "a transient phase", because the thoughts themselves are transient, very unstable, and can thus be wiped out by practice. The mind itself cannot be wiped out, because the wiper will be the mind itself. If the mind wipes out the mind, the residue will still be the mind. Thus the mind is indestructible.

8.    "There is the peaceful mind which is the supreme. When the same becomes restless, it is afflicted by thoughts. Mind is only the dynamic power (*shakti*) of the Self. There is no difference between matter and spirit. Modern science admits that all matter is energy. Energy is power or force (*shakti*). Therefore all are resolved in Siva and Shakti, i.e., the Self and the Mind."                       268

*Note*: After explaining the identity of Self and Mind, this text ends by making them Siva and Shakti, which may impress the dualists with the wrong notion of their being separate principles, as Spirit and Matter respectively, which is far from Bhagavan's intentions. In the beginning of the text the "peaceful mind" has been identified as the Supreme, that is, the Self itself. So Self and peaceful mind are convertible terms. But when, for some reason, the mind becomes "restless" or active, it manifests energy: the energy which is inherent in it turns into perceptions, thoughts, sensations, which are the phenomena, the universe. This is interpreted by the Shaktas as the creation of the "dynamic" Shakti, as distinguished from Siva, the "static" peaceful mind which is experienced in *samadhi*. This is the whole truth about Spirit and Matter. They are one and the same consciousness. The knower (or mind) develops activity inside himself, the sensations of seeing, smelling, hearing, thinking, etc., and starts enjoying the show, as if it occurs outside him. Then he is bewildered about a world and its creator — God and His Shakti, and so on. This then is the nature of the energy which science proclaims to be the constituent of the "physical" universe, the atoms. The Self is thus not only the *source* of all cosmic energy, but the Cosmic Energy *itself*. Siva is then Shakti itself.

9.  "Should I meditate on the right chest in order to meditate on the Heart?"
    Bhagavan: "The Heart is not physical. Meditation should not be on the right or the left. It should be on the Self. Everyone knows "I am". It is neither within nor without, neither on the right nor the left: 'I am' — that is all."
                                                                           273

*Note*: The noteworthy point in this text, apart from what we have already discussed, is that meditation should not be made on the physical chest, whether right or left, for that is

not the Heart at all. The 'I' is spaceless, completely free from
the association of direction or laterality. It is simply 'my being'
or 'I am', and nothing else. This sense of pure being should
be our direction in meditation and if we are unable to catch
it in the beginning we have to try again and again till we
succeed. Being present all the time in us, the intuition for it
grows rapidly, like a once-known-but-forgotten language. We
will catch up with it after some initial hesitation, which is
unavoidable. This is one of the best-cues the Master has given
us on how to recognise once again our long-forgotten
essence.

10.  "How can the world be an imagination or a thought?
Thought is a function of the mind. The mind is located
in the brain. The brain is within the skull of a human
being, who is an infinitesimal part of the universe. How
then can the universe be contained in the cells of the
brain?"
Bhagavan: "So long as the mind is considered to be an
entity of the kind described, the doubt will persist. But
what is mind? Let us consider. What is the world? It is
objects spread out in space (*akasha*). Who comprehends
it? The mind. Is not the mind which comprehends space
itself space (*akasha*)? Considering it to be ether of
knowledge (*akasha* or *jnana tattva*), there will be no difficulty
in reconciling the apparent contradiction. *Rajas* and *tamas*
operate as gross objects, etc. Thus the whole universe is
only mental."                                                451

*Note*: The question comes from a teacher of philosophy who
seems to be at sea — greatly confused even in the formulation
of the question. On the one hand he identifies man with his
body, as "an infinitesimal part of the universe", that is, the
mind with the brain; and on the other he "locates" the mind
in the brain, making the one different from the other. In

that case, Bhagavan asserts, "the doubt will persist," the problem will remain insoluble. If the brain is the mind then there will be no end to ignorance and no end to arguments. How, for example, can the insentient brain think, create, understand, smell, taste, etc.? How can Shakespeare, Gandhi and Ramana Maharshi be pieces of corruptible flesh? How do immaterial thoughts emanate from the material brain cells, and what is the relation between them? and so on. But if the mind is located in the brain, as the question puts it, then there is much hope for a solution. It will then conform to the yogic experience that the mind or the individual consciousness resides in the brain, as it has already been explained in Note 3 of this chapter. The individual is not the cerebral tissue, but the intelligent being, the consciousness which dwells in it and uses it as its instrument. Consciousness itself is pure *akasha* (ether), in which the world spreads as it appears to do in space, which itself is ether. Thus the world is nothing but consciousness or mind. That the objects appear soft or hard, hot or cold, small or big, yellow or green, sour or sweet is due to the senses which are functions of the same mind; and the world consists of nothing but what the senses give out of themselves. "Thus the whole universe is only mental." The variety of qualities which the senses inflict on our perceptions as objects are the *gunas* of which Bhagavan speaks. Thus in the manifested universe there exist nothing but qualities superimposed on the Consciousness.

## CHAPTER ELEVEN

# TRUE AND FALSE MOUNA

1.  "The silence of solitude is forced. Restrained speech in society amounts to silence. For the man then controls his speech. If the speaker is engaged otherwise speech becomes restrained. Introverted mind is otherwise active and is not anxious to speak."                                    60

*Note*: *Mouna* in the spiritual practice is a virtue sedulously cultivated. Bhagavan says that going to places of solitude for the purpose of cultivating the habit of silence is not of much value; for it is a forced state for lack of company; whereas control of the tongue in society is true silence, and thus true self-control.

The desire to speak arises in the mind, but if the mind is engaged on a subject other than that of the conversation, speech becomes greatly minimised. And the subject on which the mind of the *abhyasi* is usually engaged is the nature of the mind itself, that is, meditation, causing him reluctance to be drawn out by conversation. This is natural, not enforced, *mouna*.

Bhagavan continues:

2.  "*Mouna* as a disciplinary measure is meant for limiting the mental activities due to speech. If the mind is otherwise controlled disciplinary *mouna* is unnecessary. For *mouna* becomes natural."                                                60

*Note*: Why do *sadhakas* cultivate silence? In order to silence the mind. But this is holding the stick by the wrong end; for it is not speech that causes thinking, but thinking that causes speaking. Conversation, no doubt, provokes thinking and therefore talking, but if the mind has not been brought under control, even if there is no one to talk to, the mind will talk to itself; memory in particular will surge up and will fill the mind with thoughts of the dead past. The mind in solitude will then be in a far worse condition than in society. Memory is a more dangerous companion than the society of *sattvic* friends, who may sometimes talk on irrelevant matters, but this may prove a help to the *sadhaka*, in that it serves to break his brooding over a chain of unhappy events which are dead and gone, and whose resuscitation may depress the mind, which he endeavours to keep cheerful for the sake of a successful *sadhana*.

"If the mind is otherwise controlled," that is, by *dhyana*, *vichara* and study and by a stubborn resistance to the pressure of memory, vows of protracted silence become not only superfluous but distinctly harmful. Mental stillness is reflected in vocal stillness, which is a natural *mouna*.

3. "Vidyaranya has said that twelve years' forced *mouna* brings about absolute *mouna*, that is, it makes one unable to speak. It is more like a mute animal than otherwise. That is no *mouna*." 60

*Note*: The moral is that vows of silence and forced restraint of speech are valueless, if the mind remains restlessly active. And if it is not so active, it will have no need of compulsion — *mouna* becomes habitual.

The dig at the forced '*mouni*' who becomes "like a mute animal than otherwise", is not without justification; for cases are known when forced *mouna*, instead of making the *mouni* 'otherwise' than a "mute animal", that is, divinely inclined, it embittered rather than softened him. Years of self-violence in the end transformed itself into violence towards others. From initial humility the mind acquired arrogance and self-righteousness, alien to the character of a true seeker. The notion of his being, in his own estimation, a great *tapasvin* through years of *mouna* contributed much to this self-inflation. It does not occur to him that all animals are *mounis*, but are still far from having a controlled mind, or from being holy *tapasvins*.

4.    "Mouna is constant speech. Inactivity is constant activity."
                                                                    60

*Note*: Is this a paradox or a conundrum? It is neither if we examine it carefully. We have granted above that true silence is that of the mind, which naturally results in vocal silence. But this *mouna* has, by negation, a significance and eloquence all its own, more potent than any speech, as the silence of Sita in the next text will illustrate.

From another and truer point of view the *mouna* of the mind is not inactivity at all. The still mind is the all-dynamic pure Being, which is the plenum, the source of all phenomena, as we have studied in the previous chapters, and thus omnipotent and omniscient. To come out of this "inactive" Being to doing, to thinking, to talking is in fact dissipation of energy, a degeneration, debilitation, the cause of ignorance and misery. Therefore the "inactivity" of the still mind is immeasurably more potent than the pseudo-activity of the world of action and speech: it is "constant activity".

5.    "When Sita was asked by the wives of the Rishis who was her husband among the then assembled Rishis in the

forest, she denied each one as he by turn was pointed to her, but simply speechlessly hung down her head when Rama himself was pointed out. Her silence was eloquent. The Vedas are similarly eloquent in '*Neti*', '*Neti*' ('not this', 'not this') and then remain silent. Their silence is the Real state. This is the meaning of teaching through silence. When the source of the 'I'-thought is reached, it vanishes and what remains over is the Self." 130

*Note*: Isn't that pretty of Sita? This is an extremely apt illustration about the Self and its negation, which deserves a deeper study. Let us hang on to the '*Neti*' part of it. We say *neti* to what? Certainly to all the things we perceive and all the things we conceive — we repudiate the world altogether as false, as unintelligent. What remains as residue is the repudiator or perceiver himself but shorn of all perceptions, and therefore completely inactive — silent. This is the Self, the absolute Intelligence which perceives without being perceived, which thinks without being thought. Thus the practice of '*Neti, Neti*', of rejection, takes back the *sadhaka* to himself, as the seer of all sights, hearer of all sounds, smeller of all smells. He first looks around and begins to discard one thing after another till there remains nothing to discard, when a sudden flash of intuition, coming from within himself, from the Self itself, turns him back upon himself and reveals to him the truth of himself, as the logical residue, the pure knower, who cannot be discarded. "This is the meaning," Bhagavan avers, "of teaching through silence."

6. "*Mouna* is not closing the mouth. It is the state which transcends speech and thought. Hold some concept firmly and trace it back. By such concentration silence results. When practice becomes natural it will end in silence. Meditation without mental activity is silence."

231

*Note*: We have therefore to modify our views about vocal *mouna* and vocal *mounis*. To repeat, mental silence is the true *mouna*. It is a state by itself — the real state. How to reach that state? In the last text the *neti* method is given. Here Bhagavan gives another method, namely, holding on to only one thought, a single concept. By sticking to one thought, we will attain *mouna* in all other thoughts. Constantly hopping from one subject to another and not stopping for even a minute on a single subject is the routine work of the mind, and if this butterfly-habit can be curbed to a degree by chaining it to one subject — and one only — it is in itself a great achievement: it will lead to the eventual dropping of even the single concept, when the ultimate state of absolute *mouna* or *samadhi* will result.

What does Bhagavan mean by tracing a thought back? He means that it has to be traced to the mind from which it has arisen, for thoughts can come from nowhere but from the thinker himself: a thought of mine, for example, can come only from my own self. So that by tracing the thoughts to their source the Self can be discovered.

7.   "Is not a vow of silence helpful?"
     Bhagavan: "A vow is only a vow. It may help *dhyana* to some extent. But what is the good of keeping the mouth closed and letting the mind run riot? If the mind is occupied in *dhyana*, where is the need for speech? Nothing is as good as *dhyana*. If one takes to action with a vow of silence, what is the good of the vow?"     371

*Note*: To work, thinking is necessary, otherwise no work can be done at all, let alone successfully. But silence aims at warding off all thoughts and keeping the mind free. Therefore to take a vow of silence and continue to work is worse than contradicting oneself — it is self-delusion, let alone the ordeal it causes to the people with whom one works.

True *mouna* from speech comes naturally and spontaneously to the very few who have succeeded in killing their minds through *dhyana*. One such was the famous Mounaswami of Kumbakonam, whose very look, even in the photograph, impresses one with the awe due to a great *tapasvin* who is the personification of SILENCE. He passed over to the other side about one hundred years ago without raising a gasp or a flicker of the eyelid. He had been a *Videhamukta* even in life, when he could hardly distinguish between sleep and *samadhi*, between hunger and repletion. Food and drink used ultimately to be poured into his mouth. The half-opened eyes were hardly aware of things outside, and the body was kept by a filament of breathing for a few years. His is the natural *mouna* and himself the genuine Mouni. Sri Bhagavan himself was almost in that state the first few years of his Illumination. Temporary *mouna* for brief spells of occasional 'retreat' is quite understandable. It helps warding off intruders on one's devotions. But long-drawn-out professional *mouna* must be left strictly alone, particularly if it is accompanied by work among other people and based on a vow.

Let us always remember the Master's words that "nothing is as good as *dhyana*", which has to take the first place in the practice of *sadhana:* it produces the maximum results in the minimum time.

## CHAPTER TWELVE

# GRACE

1. "Is *Ishwara Prasad* (Divine Grace) or the jiva's own efforts necessary to attain That whence there is no return to the wheel of life and death?"

   Bhagavan: "Divine Grace is essential for Realisation. But this Grace is vouchsafed only to him who is a true devotee or a yogin, who had striven hard and ceaselessly for freedom."          24

*Note*: The inference clearly is that efforts are of the utmost importance. Grace is granted only to him who strives — "hard and ceaselessly." Thus Grace looks like a Provident Fund which is added on to the wages of him who works and earns them, and not granted to the one who does not earn. Earn more and you get a larger provident fund; earn less and you get a smaller one. Nothing is given for nothing, spiritual gifts least of all. Therefore Grace cannot be equated with efforts, for it would no longer be *Ishwara prasad*, but strictly earned wages, payment for the efforts themselves. Nor can it be equated with non-efforts, as fortuitous, unmerited gifts; for no such gifts are known to exist. God, in His infinite mercy, has contrived Grace to be a grant, a sort of bonus for genuine exertion, and as inducement to a greater exertion.

"Grace is vouchsafed only to him who is a true devotee, or a yogin, who has striven hard and ceaselessly for freedom." Let this gem idea sink in us. It comes from the highest authority about Truth in existence, and thus will have to be treasured and ceaselessly meditated on by the earnest seekers. Let him therefore, who listens to preachers who boldly proclaim God's mercy and Grace to depend on God's whims and fancies, not fall in their trap; for they are ignorant dogmatists. They imagine God to be whimsical like their own selves or weak-minded to listen to prayers. Nor should he listen to those who preach effortlessness: their words are belied by the experience and wisdom of the Master-Rishis, who, for thousands of years, gave the world its most valuable heritage — the science of Yoga.

Bhagavan calls Grace indispensable for Realisation. So it is. Provident fund, as it accumulates from day to day, year to year becomes in the end a substantial pile, which is far more valuable than wages, as it secures the ease and comforts of the subject for the rest of his life. In the case of the seeker it hails in the Supreme Guru and finally *jnana* itself, as the cumulative reward of many lives of aspiration and deliberate penance. The next text makes Grace, Guru and God identically the same.

2. "Is not the Master's Grace (*Guru Anugraha*) the result of God's Grace?" The disciple asks and the Master answers: "Why distinguish between the two? The Master is God (*Ishwara*) Himself, and not different from Him."

29

*Note*: Here Grace is the Guru, who is not other than God Himself, which, by implication, means that *Grace cannot be fully recognised till sometime after meeting the Guru, when its working becomes increasingly perceptible to the subject's consciousness.* Although throughout life one may feel something of it, yet its fullness cannot be so patently borne out till the inner transformation has taken place, due to the presence and guidance of the Guru and the practice of *sadhana*.

3.   "Does distance have any effect on Grace?" asks the American visitor, and Sri Bhagavan answers: "Time and space are within you. You are always the Self you are seeking. How do time and space affect it?"    127

*Note*: The visitor, a typical Westerner, follows the above question by the analogy of the radio broadcast, which, he says, is clearer to the nearer receiving station and dimmer to the farther. He does not indicate where he holds the transmitting station of the *Grace* he has in mind to be located — in the Pacific, the Atlantic, or in the Himalayas, or perhaps in Tiruvannamalai. If he means the last, in the person of Bhagavan, then he is right to want to be sure on this point. For the constant proximity of the Sage makes a great difference to the rapid purification of the mind and its inclination towards meditation and concentration. The opportunity to be in that proximity is an act of Grace. If Bhagavan annihilates distance in the transmission of Grace, he means that the Self is above time and space. Moreover, Bhagavan does not like to discourage the visitor, whose *prarabdha* keeps him at a distance. Yet the Grace which the visitor has in mind has a definitely determined field of action. To be always with the Master — occasional absentments excepted, — I repeat, is due to a distinctly high grade of Grace, for it quickens the maturity for Realisation. There should be no mistake about that. We have the evidence of the *Srutis*, of all *yogis*, of Bhagavan himself in many places in this work, as, for example, text 31 of the next chapter, and so on. We read again in the *Bhagavatam* (XI, xii, 1-7) that when Sri Krishna took leave of His foremost disciple Uddava before leaving this world, one of the first messages He left with him was to seek always *Sat sanga*, for, He said, nothing pleases Him more and nothing produces quicker results on the Path than the company of Sages. The company of the Guru is the greatest *Sat sanga*.

4.   "Show me Grace."
     Bhagavan: "Grace always is, and is not given."          133

5.   "There are disciples of Bhagavan who have had His Grace
     and realised without any considerable difficulty. I too
     wish to have that Grace."
     Bhagavan: "Grace is within you. If it is external it is
     useless. Grace is the Self. You are never out of its
     operation. If you remember Bhagavan, you are prompted
     by the Self to do so. Is that not Grace? Is not Grace
     already there? That is the stimulus, that is the response,
     that is Grace."                                         251

*Note*: The second questioner is a lady, probably a Highness
on the *gadi* of some Central Indian State, who cannot retire
to the Ashram and be always near the Master. She assumes
that some of Bhagavan's disciples had His Grace "without
considerable difficulty" and realised the Self, so that she too
must have it without considerable difficulty, notwithstanding
the distance of her residence from Him. It is seldom safe to
rely on conjectures. Hard exertion, as we have observed, is
necessary to earn Grace, which ever abounds, because it
"always is". Simple requests will not suffice, because Grace is
"not given".

Grace, Bhagavan asserts, is not external, for "if it is
external it is useless": it could then be purchased even without
merits. Grace is internal and must therefore be secured by
merits born of efforts. Those who cannot exert must be
satisfied with crumbs or small morsels. Lack of time and of
favourable circumstances are the enemies of *sadhana*. They
may be due to *prarabdha*, yet Bhagavan asserts elsewhere
that *prarabdha* cracks under the hammer-strokes of effort.
Practice remains in the last analysis of paramount necessity
to the serious-minded seeker. (See text 27 in the next
chapter.)

6.  "I am unable to concentrate to have peace by myself. I am in search of a force to help me," asks the visitor, and the Master replies: "Yes, that is called Grace. Individually we are incapable because the mind is weak. Grace is necessary. *Sadhu seva* (service of saints) is meant only for it. Just as a weak man comes under the control of a stronger one, so does the weak mind come easily under control in the presence of the stronger-minded saint. There is, however, nothing new to get. That which is, is only Grace, there is nothing else."                                287

*Note*: The questioner is in great mental distress, which by himself he is unable to overcome. He has tried to meditate, has read the *Gita*, the *Upanishads* and all the books of this Ashram, yet he remains restless, and so he needs Bhagavan's help. What medicine can cure such a mind? You cannot teach him, for he has learnt everything that needs learning. You cannot talk him out of his distress by any means, for, we may be sure, he has talked to himself times without number about it. The only remedy left for him, Bhagavan suggests, is service of saints, which implies a long residence in their company, which alone is capable of normalising a distraught mental state. That is why the scriptures advise *Sat sanga* to soothe shattered nerves and eliminate ignorance. There is really no other way. Even if one is a millionaire who can afford to take a round-the-world trip and drown his worries in the seas he crosses, or in the wonders he meets abroad, on his return to his old environments he will resume his old worries, as he will the wearing of his old clothes. This is only a temporary device, but the company of saints transforms the inner vision for the better and for good. By increasing the tendency to introversion one draws nearer to the peace and bliss of the Self. Meditation apart, the mere proximity of a saint imparts happiness to all around.

7.   "Is not Grace the gift of the Guru?"
Bhagavan: "God, Grace and Guru are synonymous
terms. They are eternal and immanent. If a Guru thinks
that he can bestow the Self, which is already present, he
does not deserve the name. The books say that there are
various kinds of *diksha* or initiations — *hasta, sparsa,
chakshu, mano*, etc. The Guru makes some rites with fire,
water, *japa, mantras*, etc. and calls these fantastic
performances *dikshas*, as if the disciple becomes ripe only
after them.
"What did Dakshinamurti, the Supreme Guru do? He
remained simply silent and the doubts of the disciples
were dispelled: they lost their individualities. This is *jnana*,
and not all the verbiage usually associated with it.
"Silence is most potent in its effects. The *Shastras*, however
voluminous and emphatic they may be, fall far short in
their effect. The Guru is quiet and peace pervades all.
His silence is vaster and more effective than all the
*Shastras* put together. These questions arise because of
the feeling (among some) that, having been here for so
long, heard so much, exerted so hard, one has not gained
anything. The work proceeding within is not apparent,
though the Guru is always within you."             398

*Note*: The three Gs is a formula which can he always
remembered as a trinity in unity — the fount of Divine Mercy
for the redemption of erring man. Thus Guru is Grace, so
that to ask Grace from the external Guru is meaningless.
In our extroverted vision we imagine the body of the Guru
to be the Guru Himself and Grace to be communicable, that
is, coming from an external object; whereas in fact Grace
springs up from inside the seeker himself. Bhagavan
deprecates all external vehicles of Grace as well as pseudo-
gurus, who claim the conferring of Grace orally through
whispered *mantras*, fire and water. Bhagavan dubs these
useless rites, termed "initiations", as fantastic, and very

rightly too. They are cheap stuff, which the man of purity and spiritual stamina summarily rejects. Those who claim ability and authority to confer Grace, or, what is the same, the Self, do not know the Self — "they do not deserve the name of Gurus," Bhagavan says.

When we seriously cogitate over these remarks of Bhagavan in the light of our own experience and reason, we find them to be true to the hilt. Spirituality-loaded *Mantras* have been whispered in the ears of millions upon millions for ages and have resulted in almost nothing, except perhaps in the temporary imaginary elation of the "initiates" for which they have often to pay in money, service, etc. In the West, we have analogous rites which are supposed to work miracles on the millions of their partaking devotees. What is the result? *Adhikara* (natural maturity) alone counts: it comes to those who do not take part in rites and "initiations" as well as to those who do.

Silence, Bhagavan continues, is far more helpful in the spiritual path than all the big tomes of the *Shastras* and scholarship, for the Self is the silent witness of all things, and is in everyone, and thus can be attained only through silence of the mind. To be It we have to be silent like It.

Hence Bhagavan asserts that those who stay long in the Ashram must not imagine themselves in the least neglected. Grace, as the Self, works silently and imperceptibly. They are soaked in it, and are every minute steadily advancing towards the glorious experience of *It*, which is the immediate goal of all genuine *sadhakas*.

CHAPTER THIRTEEN

# DHARANA, DHYANA AND SAMADHI

1. "How to transcend the mind?" The Master answers: "Mind is by nature restless. Begin liberating it from its restlessness: give it peace; make it free from distractions; train it to look inward; make this a habit. This is done by ignoring the external world and removal of the obstacles to the peace of mind."                    26

*Note*: In the previous chapters we discussed some of the ways of transcending the mind to reach the Self. Here Bhagavan recommends tranquillity to begin with; for we cannot proceed with the *vichara* when the turbulence of the mind is at its height, any more than we can navigate our ship in a stormy sea.

We must first steer it to some shelter till calm prevails, when we can ply our oars and reach safely our destination.

People complain that the world is too storm-tossed to give them peace. Bhagavan suggests to them to ignore the world, so that if it is responsible for the restlessness of their minds, the latter will acquire calmness by degrees. But if they will not, it will prove that the storm is inside and not outside them. Then they will have to look within: this is *vichara*.

As meditation is of utmost importance in this yoga, this chapter contains an extensive selection of hints on it. It goes without saying that the working of men's minds differs one from the other, so that it is not possible to frame yogic rules which can apply to all of them. A Guru is necessary to guide each disciple according to his peculiar circumstances. At best only hints can be given to the general aspirants to light their path and instil in them the requisite confidence to tread it. Such hints are found here in adequate number.

As a first step Bhagavan suggests mental quiescence, for it is not possible to come from the hectic activities of ordinary life and plunge straight into meditation, and expect it to succeed. Much preparation has to be made through study, reflection, and *sat sanga* to transform the worldly *vasanas* into those of the *sadhana*, when the mind will, of its own accord, be inclined "to look inward".

It is therefore to the advantage of the practicants not to attempt meditation straightaway, but first to acquire mastery of Bhagavan's teaching and learn how to direct the meditation to attain its aim. This time will not be wasted, for profound study not only takes away the worldly *vasanas* but it is *dharana* (concentration) itself, the stepping-stone to a successful meditation (*dhyana*).

Bhagavan develops the subject:

> 2.　"External contacts — contacts with objects other than itself — make the mind restless. Loss of interests in the not-Self (*vairagya*) is the first step. Then the habits of introspection and concentration follow, ending in *samadhi*."　　26

*Note*: Bhagavan here sheds light on the relation of the mental restlessness to the world. He distinguishes between the mind itself and the external objects, which he calls "other than the mind", i.e., between the Self, which we are seeking, and the not-Self, which we have to abandon, namely, the world of the sense-objects, which is ever restless. He makes us see the direct opposition of the latter to the former — the not-

Self to the Self. If we cleave to the not-Self, it stands to reason that we cannot hope to get at the Self, and then we shall not be justified in grieving over our failure, or blaming it on God or on the Guru. Cleave to the world and you are lost to the Self, at least for the period of your cleaving. Cleave to the Self and you are lost to the world, rather the world is lost to you. We cannot hope to see the light if we stubbornly hold on to the darkness: the one is repugnant to the other. If we abandon the one we will enjoy (or suffer) the other to the full. This is plain common sense.

But this may be misunderstood as advocating the desertion of one's home, wife, children and other obligations. Nothing is farther from the truth. This sort of interpretation leads to perdition, making the bleakness of one's prospects more bleak. We have seen how Bhagavan discourages escapism, which is, truly speaking, not *vairagya* but callous egotism. Rational seekers do not make this mistake, or argue that since the Self is alone real, all family and domestic encumbrances are mere dream, which need not be taken seriously. This argument resembles that of the foolish disciples in the story, who dropped their Rishi in a deep pit to bring his teaching of *Maya* to ridicule. They thought, the story goes, he would plead to take him out of the pit and would thus repudiate *Maya*. They called out to him from the top of the pit derisively: "Well Sir, now you can tell us if the world is an illusion: but please remember where you are." The Rishi undaunted feebly answered from the abysmal darkness: "The world is illusion, but not this pit," meaning thereby that although the world is an illusion, the suffering in the pit is, like the dream suffering, real, while it lasts. So, although the world is the not-Self, an illusion, the suffering which we inflict upon others, our family in this case, is genuine and becomes the cause of our own future suffering, for the Self

is one. Sri Krishna, the Self, speaks to Arjuna of the deluded
and arrogant people who cause trouble to others: "These
malignant ones hate Me in the bodies of others and in their
own." (*Bhagavad Gita*, XVI, 18).

Bhagavan in this text asks us "to lose interest in the
not-Self", which implies detachment in the performance of
duty, freedom from that clinging passion for the family and
for possessions. Giving up infatuation for the family is one
thing and giving up the family itself is quite another. Abjuring
this passion, which is not the same as the negative escapism,
causes mental calmness. This is the true significance of
*vairagya*, which can be attained through the analysis of *vichara*;
for (Bhagavan continues):

3.  "An examination of the ephemeral nature of the external
    phenomena leads to *vairagya*. Hence enquiry is the first
    and foremost step to be taken, which will result in
    contempt for wealth, fame, ease, pleasure, etc. The 'I'-
    thought becomes clearer for inspection."               27

*Note*: This is a clear direction for the attainment of *vairagya*.
These two texts practically conclude as follows: the 'I' has so
far been loaded with things that are not 'I' — with wealth,
fame, power, family relationships, social status, individual
names and titles, with various *koshas* (bodies), etc., which are
temporary — "ephemeral." Take away all this superfluous
load by enquiry and discrimination, and the 'I' will remain
alone as the eternal Self. This is true *vairagya*. Therefore the
renunciation must be with respect to this load, these useless
trappings, which hide the true nature of the 'I' from our
vision by their glamour and their peculiar appeals. *Vichara*
unloads the 'I' and restores to us the fullness of the being
and its eternal freedom, even though we may retain the body
and all human relationships. We shall then become ourselves

in the full sense of the term. We will have then proved to ourselves that in the long run the *plus* works out to *minus* — the gain is actually a loss. Wealth and possessions, so long as we retain a passion for them, are in fact subtractions rather than additions. This is the paradox of the life of the body and the world.

Bhagavan now turns to other methods than the *vichara*.

4.  "If, however, the aspirant is not temperamentally suited to the *vichara marga*, he must develop *bhakti* (devotion) to an Ideal — maybe God, Guru, Humanity in general, ethical laws, or even the idea of Beauty. When one of these has taken possession of the individual, other attachments grow weaker and dispassion (*vairagya*) develops. Thus *ekagrata* (concentration) grows simultaneously and imperceptibly.

    "In the absence of *vichara* and *bhakti*, control of breath (*pranayama*) may be tried. This is known as *Yoga marga*. If the breath is held the mind cannot jump at its pets — the objects. Thus there is rest for the mind so long as the breath is held. The mind improves by practice and becomes finer, just as the razor's edge is sharpened by stropping."                                                          27

*Note*: *Vichara* is not therefore the only method of practice to begin with. There are some who do not know how to enquire and how to analyse their thoughts and emotions. They begin and end with the empirical 'I'. How to find its root, and how to follow up the 'I'-thought, is a problem to which they find no solution. To such the *vichara marga* remains infructuous — an obstacle rather than a help. Bhagavan advises them to take to *bhakti*, that is, to develop a devotion to an Ideal, even though that Ideal may be as concrete as the service of humanity or a virtue for which they aspire. If *bhakti* is sufficiently developed, *vairagya* and concentration follow as a matter of course. If devotion to an Ideal is also lacking, the seeker may resort to *japa* or *pranayama* to arrest the restlessness of the mind. All these practices specifically aim at stopping the *vritti*, the ceaseless modification, the wanderings of the mind, so that the latter may be nailed to itself and may eventually cognise its own native state. Mental diffusiveness resembles a mixture of gold dust with sand, earth, ashes and dirt of all sorts. Concentration (*dharana*) and meditation (*dhyana*) are the sieve which sifts the gold dust from the others. They churn the *nadis* (nerves) along which consciousness flows to the whole body and track them down to their source, the Heart. Relaxation of the nervous system then takes place, denoting the ebbing of the consciousness from the *nadis* back to the Heart. The ebbs and flows of the consciousness, which constant practice renders increasingly perceptible to the meditator, gradually loosen the consciousness from the body and end by separating them in *samadhi*, so that the *sadhaka* is enabled to perceive the consciousness alone and pure. This is the Self, God the Absolute.

Hence concentration is recommended in every form of spiritual practice and in every school of Yoga. It is brought about by *bhakti*, which starts and keeps going the fire of *tapas*. *Bhakti* is thus all-inclusive and it is highest in the complete surrender which the Yogin achieves in the path of *jnana* and *vichara*. Some practicants find it easier to take to *pranayama* to control the mind. That is also an effective method of realisation, provided they do not get involved in the *chakras* but end in the Heart.

5.    "What are the steps in the practical *sadhana*?"
      The Master: "They depend on the qualifications and the nature of the seeker. If you are doing idol worship, you should go on with it: it will lead you to concentration. Get

one-pointed, and all will come out right. People think
that Liberation is far away and should be sought out. They
are wrong. It is only knowing the Self within oneself.
Concentrate and you will get it. The mind is the cycle of
births and deaths. Go on practising and concentration
will be as easy as breathing. That will be the crown of your
achievements." 31

*Note*: Spiritual practices are therefore purely individual,
depending on one's temperament, intellectual abilities,
modes of thinking, peculiar circumstances and other
emotional and spiritual factors. But whatever these may be,
a resort to concentration, as we have seen above, is a *sine qua
non*, for which any convenient instrument may be used.
Patanjali's *Yoga Sutras* and the Upanishads describe some of
the methods without exhausting them; for they are as many
as the seekers themselves.

Liberation, Bhagavan tells us, is not the acquisition of
a new situation or qualification, but only of the most correct
point of view about oneself, which is already here and now.
We possess a false view of our identity, like the proverbial
millionaire who stubbornly imagined himself to be a
miserable pauper, and acted as if he were truly such, and
thus perpetuated his wretchedness. We are immortal, but
imagine ourselves to be mortal, and act according to this
belief. We are nothing but the Supreme Intelligence or Pure
knowledge, the knower of all things, thinker, feeler, conceiver,
creator, and not mere chemical compounds, mere flesh,
blood, bones, bile and mucus, which hardly bear an aesthetic
examination. There is a pronounced discrepancy, which
escapes us, between the body-I belief and the revulsion we
feel at the exposure of the body's internal parts. We love
ourselves most, and if the body is us, how is it that we cannot
tolerate this exhibition? We hardly need a highly developed

analytical faculty to discover this patent incongruity. Once we disentangle the intelligent in us from the unintelligent body by practice, we are liberated that very instant. So liberation is there for the asking, completely at our disposal, if we but make up our mind and act with resolute determin- ation. Self-"real"-isation therefore simply means discovering to be "real" that — our selves — which we have so far taken to be unreal and mortal: "It is only knowing the Self within oneself."

6.    "If you go the way of your thoughts you will be carried away by them and will find yourself in an endless maze. But if you trace back the source of thoughts these will disappear and the Self alone will remain. In fact there is no inside or outside for the Self. They are the projections of the ego. The Self is pure and absolute."                                  13

*Note*: Thoughts include sensations, pet notions, all habits of the mind (*vasanas*), — the sense of 'I' and 'mine', etc. If we thoughtlessly let ourselves go and yield to the promptings of these habits and instincts, we will be swamped, literally involved in an "endless maze", which will tend to keep the ego firmly fixed in *avidya*, suffering the consequences of its ignorance. "Slimming" becomes necessary. Shed the *vasanas:* track them down to their source by investigation, and you are bound to reach the Self. You will never go astray, for all thoughts are rooted in the Self, as all the branches of a tree are rooted in the earth.

7.    "If the origin is *sat* only, why is it not felt?" Bhagavan: "The salt in lump is visible, but invisible in solution; still it is cognised by its taste. Similarly *sat* (or truth), though not perceived by the intellect is still realisable in other ways. How? Just as a man who has been robbed and blindfolded by robbers and thrown in a jungle

enquires his way and returns home, so also the *ajnani*
who is blinded by ignorance enquires his way from the
*Jnani* and returns to his source."     108

*Note*: *Sat* "in lump" is Brahman, the Self, alone and pure. It
is experienced as concentrated consciousness in *samadhi*.
Once the senses are out again, the concentrated consciousness ("in lump") spreads out to the whole body and becomes
a "solution", and thus imperceptible. Yet the *Jnani* knows it
by "its taste". This is a delightful metaphor. What we want
now is to "taste" it in its *lumpiness*, so that we may distinguish
it from the body in which it is now in "solution" — in an
indistinguishable state. Bhagavan advises us to enquire from
him who has tasted it in both the states, as the blindfolded
man finds his way home with the help of those whose eyes
are open. Robbers (the senses) have stolen the knowledge
of the Self from us by blinding us with the world illusion.
We have now to resort to the Master who has found the
Self, so that we too may see and "taste" it again, as we used
to do before the cruel burglary had taken place.

8.    "Please help me to realise the Self. It is no use reading
      books."
      Bhagavan answers, "Quite so. If the Self be found in books,
      it would have been realised long ago. Is it not a wonder
      that we should seek the Self in books? Can it be found
      there? Of course books have impelled the question." 117

*Note*: Bhagavan is, of course, right to be satirical about
finding the Self in books. To lose oneself and then search for
it in books resembles the case of the proverbial princess,
who all along carries her necklace round her neck but goes
in search of it everywhere outside her person. A single look
in the mirror would have sufficed. The mirror of the Self is

the 'I', our own being. How can books act as its mirror? Sound books can only induce the search and suggest ways and means. Even then we should have to act upon the suggestions in our own mind, which more often than not we do not. Why? We have no time, you know.

9.   "The *Srutis* speak of the Self as being of the size of the thumb, the tip of the hair, a spark, subtler than the subtle, etc., etc. They have no foundation in fact. It is only Being. It is simply Being. People desire to see it as a blazing light, etc. How can it be? It is neither light nor darkness. It is only as it is. It cannot be defined. The best definition for it is 'I am that I am'."                      122

*Note*: That settles it: we are not to take literally all the descriptions of the Self found here and there. If we do, then we will be giving form to the formless, name to the nameless, and attributes to the attributeless. All objective descriptions and comparisons of the Self are meaningless, and must stop at a point not too far away. Bhagavan does not wish to slight the *Srutis*, because he himself very often quotes them. What he decries is only the lack of uniformity and cohesion which almost always confound and confuse the casual student and biased theologian who finds in them a vast field for adverse propaganda. The beginner feels himself honestly lost in what appears to be a maze of inconsistencies and exaggerations, as witness these descriptions of the Self. The *Jnani* knows how to tackle the *Upanishads*. The veteran seeker likewise skims much of their cream, according to his intuitive maturity. The others take them literally and allow their imagination to run riot, or hold to their letter tenaciously but allow the spirit to slip through their fingers.

Bhagavan is keen that we should have a notion of the Self which is divested of all analogies and sensuous descriptions. The Self is the pure Being. To be, by its very definition, means to exist, which negates nonexistence. Being therefore means eternal existence, which can be said of only an indestructible substance. But all objective things are destructible, being insentient. Therefore eternal existence can be predicated of only the be-ing which is pure sentience. This we call the Infinite Self or Supreme Consciousness which transcends all objectivity. What description or analogy can therefore fit it? Bhagavan finds a single definition which can do so, namely, 'I am that I am,' that is, the "indefinable Being."

10. "One should not be content with mere discipleship, initiation, ceremony of surrender, etc. These are external phenomena. Never forget the Truth underlying all phenomena."     133

*Note*: This should be read side by side with the last note of the last chapter — the chapter on Grace — which also refers to ceremonies and initiations. Those who attach importance to these performances are welcome to continue them, but they should know that "initiations" are not indispensable for spiritual progress. They come nowhere before the direct investigation and meditation of the *yoga sadhana*. Ceremonies are phenomena and thus have a magical value to those who believe in the phenomena. The seeker has to learn to do without them and concentrate on the eternal truth which underlies all phenomena and which can be found nowhere but inside his own heart. He who worships through ceremonies and *mantras* remains in illusion and under the influence of the *devas* who are supposed to preside over the *mantras*. Sri Krishna says in the *Gita* that he who worships *devas* goes to the *devas*, but His devotee goes direct to Him, the Supreme Atman.

If the *mantras* of initiation can give Liberation, even our "dumb brethren" can secure it. There is, of course, nothing against a little ceremony in certain phases of life, e.g., birth, marriage, death, taking *sannyasa*, to give an air of sanctity to the function and impress the people concerned, but to believe that it has more in it than that, is to cross into the world of illusion. But the *mantras* which are used as *japa* in the spiritual practice are entirely different. That is the *sadhana* proper and many *sadhakas* are greatly helped by them. They have no connection with any *deva* and lead eventually to the Self.

> 11.  "What is the difference between meditation and distraction?" Bhagavan: "When there are thoughts it is distraction. When thoughts are absent it is meditation. However, meditation is only practice as distinguished from the real state of peace."                                68

*Note*: The last sentence means that although in meditation the mind is expected to be free from thoughts, it is not Realisation itself, which is the state of Peace, but still the stage of practice for Realisation. Meditation means attempts to gain freedom from thoughts, and distraction is the inability to gain that freedom. Thinking, of whatever nature and quality, is therefore distraction, ignorance and the cause of suffering. But to imagine that in the advanced meditation there is no peace is wrong, because as thoughts relax their pressure on the mind, disturbance proportionately decreases, which is what is experienced as peace, repose, mental ease and comfort, a foretaste of the peace absolute of the Self which will follow.

> 12.  "For whom is the blank? Find out. You cannot deny yourself at any time. The Self is ever there and continues in all states."                                13

*Note*: This is an answer to an enquirer who either sees blank in meditation or goes to sleep. It is the constant complaint of beginners that when thoughts stop the substratum or Self is not perceived. One has not yet become firmly established in the practice to be sensitive enough to intuit the substratum of thought. To *seek* a blank is to think a blank, which is, again, a thought. Thus the free mind has not yet been attained. Instead of having an active thought one has then a passive one, which is still a thought. I call it a passive thought because it is not of a well-defined conception, or sensuous perception — of a sound, or smell, or taste — but a thought nevertheless, of which the meditator is well-aware, otherwise he would not speak of it. At this point an occasion arises for a mildly increased alertness, which may have a successful result. It is this: the perception of the blank is obvious then, but there stands, as if in the background, though in fact right in the centre of, or all about the experience, the seer of the blank. If this is remembered at that moment and the attention switches off from the blank on to this seer — oneself — not the body of the seer, but the consciousness that sees the blank, one stands a great chance of perceiving It, or at least beginning to apprehend Its nature. By constant repetition direct perception of It is bound to result. This is Self-Knowledge.

13. "The mind must be introverted (in *dhyana*) and kept active in its pursuit. Sometimes it happens when the eyes are closed latent thoughts rush forth with great vigour. It may also be difficult to introvert the mind with the eyes open. It requires strength of mind to do so. The mind is contaminated when it takes in objects. Otherwise it is pure." 61

*Note*: Should the eyes be open or closed in meditation? This text gives the answer, which means "either way". Generally the eyes are kept closed to prevent ocular experiences which are far more disturbing than those of the other sensory organs. The important thing to remember is that the mind should be kept preoccupied with the meditation, and never be allowed to be either sluggish or to stray at will without restraint. It has to be tied to the focal point of the meditation. Yet stray it will, it must, which should not worry the meditator, who has simply to be alert enough to be aware of this straying and to bridle it back immediately, giving it no scope to go out of his control. This last happens when the meditator gets involved in a subject in which he is now, or was once, interested, so that he entirely forgets himself and the work on which he is now engaged. Memory is to blame for it: it should be carefully watched and firmly restrained.

14.   "*Sphurana* is felt on several occasions, such as in fear, excitement, etc. Although it is always and all over, yet it is felt at a particular centre and on particular occasions. It is also associated with antecedent causes and confounded with the body. Whereas it is also alone and pure: it is the Self. If the mind is fixed on the *Sphurana* and one senses it continually and automatically, it is Realisation."     62

*Note*: This is a fascinating subject like the sensation of the *sphurana* itself. Obviously the questioner has an experience of it to impel him to seek elucidation about it. There are those who look askance at it: they are of course mistaken. *Sphurana* is defined (in brackets, not here) as a "kind of indescribable but palpable sensation in the Heart centre", which Bhagavan tells us "is felt on several occasions" and "all over". Those who first sense it in meditation become thrilled by it, and if they happen to have read or known nothing about it, they get puzzled at what it all means. Bhagavan clarifies the position. The apparent discrepancy in its location as "all over" and the "Heart centre" is, apart from the unpredictable psychological occasions mentioned in the text, due to the degree of firmness in, or proximity to the Self at the moment. In the beginning when the Heart has not yet revealed itself, it is felt "all over", as it always is, particularly on the right side of the body. But with constant practice its diffusion gradually diminishes and fixes itself in the Heart, nay, it becomes the Heart itself. The diffusion of consciousness "all over" is the consciousness "in solution" of text 7, in this chapter. Between the first sensing of the *sphurana* and the discovery of the Heart, which is the Self proper — the consciousness "in lump" — there is only a short lag of time, so that those who are so fortunate as to begin to feel it, take heart at the imminence of the Supreme Experience. Thereafter it continues to be felt — it is then *mukti* itself, Bhagavan says, which he confirms in the next text.

15. "Again, *Sphurana* is the foretaste of Realisation. It is pure." 62

*Note*: This is encouraging to the followers of the path of *vichara* to know that the Supreme Consciousness sends its harbinger to welcome them a good time in advance — a harbinger which in the end turns out to be the Host Himself, the Supreme Lord of the House, nay, Host, Guest and Home all in one (text 32).

16. "I have faith in *murti dhyana* (worship of form). Will this help me to gain *jnana*?"
Bhagavan: "Surely it will. *Upasana* helps concentration of mind. Then the mind is free from other thoughts and is full of the meditated form. The mind becomes it — and thus quite pure. Then think who is the worshipper. The answer is 'I'-the Self. So the Self is gained ultimately." 63

*Note*: So long as the mind is amenable to control, the means of doing it is immaterial. Once the mental diffusion is restrained, the worship of form (*upasana*) will automatically change over to the *vichara*, that is, investigation into the identity of the worshipper himself. This is unavoidable, for the reason of the fact that however dear the worshipped form may be, it cannot be dearer than one's own Self, and secondly it is changeable, whereas the subject, the worshipper himself, is changeless, as the witness of all change and all objects. Complete satisfaction is never obtained till the knowledge of oneself as the changeless and absolute conscious existence takes place, which will compel the *vichara* by a natural necessity.

It is granted that the worshipped form is *sattvic* — ideally pure — to be capable of inducing alike purity in the worshipper's mind.

17.  "All are agreed that the *jiva is*. Let us find out the *jiva* first Then there will be time to find out if it should merge in the Supreme, is a part thereof, or remains different from it. Let us not forestall the conclusion. Keep an open mind, dive within and find out the Self. The truth will itself dawn on you. Why should you determine beforehand if the finality is unity or duality, absolute or qualified?" 63

*Note*: The context is the relation of Monism to Dualism — whether they interchange, whether one should begin with duality and end with unity, etc. Bhagavan argues that all that is unnecessary to know beforehand. All schools, whether dualistic, monistic or qualified monistic, agree that the basis of their creeds is the *jiva*, whose existence all admit. Since the *jiva* is undeniable, one should start with it? which is what our monistic school does in its enquiry about the nature of the seeker's own self. The rest will of its own accord unfold itself till the end, when one will be in a position to judge for oneself which of the three schools is right. At the present stage the question should be allowed to hang fire, for it is not capable of solution.

18.  "What if one meditates incessantly without *karma* (without action)?" The Master replies: "Try and see. The *vasanas* will not let you. *Dhyana* comes only step by step with the gradual weakening of the *vasanas* by the Grace of the Master."                                                                 80

*Note*: By *vasanas* is meant the habits of the mind, which ceaselessly pop up as thoughts, like the ceaseless waves of the ocean. Memory is the storehouse of the *vasanas* and thus the worst enemy of a quiescent mind.

By action we are not to understand manual work alone, but also thinking. Action results only from thinking. It is its manifestation in the phenomenal world, the execution of its commands. Thus in the last analysis work proves to be nothing but *vasanas*. The control of the *vasanas* can be achieved by a slow process, through constant practice, helped by the presence of the Master, which gradually files away the dirt of the mind and strengthens it. *Guru sanga* is the greatest of all blessings if accompanied by determined efforts.

Studying the tricks of memory is a very helpful practice, which will result in keeping one on one's guard, against its insidious pressure on the whole course of the *sadhana*. Retrospection, excepting as it has a direct bearing on the *vichara*, is always a drawback in this practice, for there is generally nothing uplifting in the experiences of a less mature age. More often than not it rouses sorrowful memories, regrets and passion, which have to be thrown into the limbo, rather than be resuscitated in a mind which is looking upwards, towards the light that never dims.

19. "He who instructs an ardent seeker to do this or that (work) is not a true master. The seeker is already afflicted by his activities and wants peace and rest. He wants cessation of his activities. Instead he is told to do something in addition to, or in place of, his other activities."     601

20. "Activity is creation; activity is the destruction of one's inherent happiness. If it is advocated, the adviser is not a master but a killer. Either the Creator (Brahma) or Death (Yama) may be said to have come in the guise of such a master. He cannot liberate the aspirant but strengthens his fetters."     601

*Note*: No one can deny that Bhagavan is very firm in decrying work by the aspirant, because of the reports he receives from some of the meditating disciples, who have been asked to work as service to him, the Guru. Bhagavan places meditation on the highest level, as the noblest of work. He discourages burdening "ardent" *sadhakas*, who stand in need of mental quiescence, with extraneous work in the name of service to the master. Work is worldly and needs a certain amount of attention, if it is to be well done, which can only take the aspirant's mind in a direction opposite to that of the *sadhana*. Ashrams have, no doubt, to be run by devotees as honorary workers, but these must be selected from non-meditating, or less "ardent" residents. Some such institutions go so far as to admit no non-workers on their premises, for all must work, they insist, to promote the ideals of their peculiar brand of Truth. To Bhagavan "this adviser is not a master but a killer". One almost hears the voice of Vyasadeva in the *Bhagavata Purana* condemning action for the devotee in four long chapters (10/13, Book XI). Shankara adds his quota in stanza 3 of his *Atma Bodha* which says that "Action cannot destroy ignorance, for it is not hostile to it. Knowledge alone can destroy it, as light destroys darkness."

As for worldly action, Bhagavan is emphatic that it destroys happiness, for it is created, supported and perpetuated by ignorance. It is caused by desire and ends in bondage, which is misery in essence. Bhagavan characterises the preacher of action as the embodiment of Yama, the Lord of Death, which is the strongest language he can use against the promoters of action.

21. "'Who am I?' is the best *japa*. What can be more concrete than the Self? It is within each one's experience every moment. Why should he try to catch (as *japa*) an outside thing, leaving out the Self? Let each one try to find out the known Self, instead of searching for the unknown beyond."     81

*Note*: This is an answer to the demand of an American visitor for a concrete idea like *japa*, *dhyana*, etc., to which one can hold in the search of what he calls the "Light", rather than being merely told that if thoughts cease the Self alone remains. The visitor does not seem to have understood the implication of the self-enquiry. In the first instance he does not identify the Self or 'I' with the "Light" or Reality which he is seeking. Bhagavan tells him that the quest 'Who am I' is the best *japa*. For the whole *sadhana* consists of nothing but knowing it, which once done, our work is at an end. The visitor has not yet learnt the fact that the 'I' is the only intelligence existing in this vast universe, and all else is as dead as a door nail, incapable of making itself known by its own light. The light of the 'I' alone can reveal it. No object or world can exist by itself apart from this 'I' (of which it is a thought) as its container as well as knower. The 'I' is the only immanent element in all our experiences whatever. We know it most as our own Self, and because we do not perceive it as we perceive all other things, we are now seeking to know it *absolutely* in all these spiritual practices, through the guidance of the Master, for it is pure spirit or pure knowledge. What other *japa* can be more useful and more concrete than it — our 'I', — Bhagavan asks?

The next few texts will shed more light on Bhagavan's meaning of the quest "Who am I".

22. "Please say how I shall realise the 'I'. Am I to make the *japa* 'Who am I?'
Bhagavan: "No *japa* of the kind is meant."
Visitor: Am I to think 'Who am I?'
Bhagavan: "Hold the 'I'-thought and find its *moola* (source)."                                              486

23. "Enquiry 'Who am I?' means finding the source of 'I'. When that is found, that which you seek is accomplished."
                                                                          67

*Note*: The above two texts should leave no doubt in the mind of the *abhyasi* (the practicant) about Bhagavan's use of the enquiry 'Who am I?'. It is neither a slogan nor a mantra, but an intense enquiry into one's own nature. That is why this method is called *vichara* (enquiry). Although sometimes he uses the epithet *japa* for it, as in text 21 above, he does not mean it to be a mechanical incantation, but an actual investigation in the 'I''s real nature, which he further develops in the next text.

24. "The One Infinite Unbroken Whole becomes aware of itself as 'I'. This is its original name. All other names, e.g., OM, etc., are later growths. Liberation means only to remain aware of the Self. The *Mahavakya* 'I am Brahman' is its authority. Though the 'I' is always experienced, yet one's attention has to be drawn to it. Then only knowledge dawns. Hence is the need for the teaching of the Upanishads and the Sages."                              92

*Note*: Bhagavan takes us here to the genesis of the 'I', which is the very first self-awareness of the "Unbroken whole". It is the name the Self gave to itself and precedes all other names of the Absolute. When it is realised as such by direct experience, Liberation is said to have been achieved. *Yoga Vasishta* calls this first self-awareness by the Absolute as the first stir of thinking in Brahman, like the first wave of a calm ocean from within itself.

There are two ways of being self-aware: objectively and subjectively. If I stand on one side and on the other stand others and the world — I in opposition to you — then the 'I' is the objective body: a part of the world of multiplicity. But if I am aware of myself as pure awareness, it is subjective self-awareness, when the world is totally absent. The former 'I' being objective, is a mere thought — an 'I'-thought — and should be destroyed, like all other thoughts, in order that the 'I' may cease to be a thought and may turn upon itself as the one who is aware of the thought, through the help of the Guru or Scriptures. This is the meaning of "one's attention has to be drawn to it". In other words, the 'I' will cease to be a thought, and will remain only the Consciousness 'I am', which is the *Mahavakya* to which the text refers. This is Liberation itself.

By "its original name" and "later growths" in the text above, we are not to understand that the 'I' has a beginning and a progress towards an end. Such an interpretation goes against the absolutism of Advaita, and against all that we have so far studied. It refers only to the genesis of this dream, which we call the *jiva* and the universe; the genesis of the 'I'-thought, of the 'I' imagining itself a part of a world of multiplicity.

25. "So long as there is a knower there is knowledge — knowledge of all kinds: direct, inferential, intellectual,

etc. Let the knower vanish and they will all simultaneously vanish. Their validity stands and falls with him."

93

*Note*: The knower comes before his knowledge. Knowledge of
various kinds is nothing but the world's multiplicity. Thus the
world comes after, and depends on, the knower, with whom "it
stands and falls". Without the seer there can be no seen, because
the seen is a mere thought in the seer, who is not a thought at
all; for if he were, he would disappear with his thoughts, and
there would remain no one to tell the tale; no one to speak of
yesterday or of last year's events. Our life consists mainly of
memory, of remembered persons, scenes and events, which
proves our fixity in a changeable world. We are the fixed
observation post, as it were, and all things, from birth to death,
march past us. They come and go, but we, the 'I', remain ever.
Even if the body is cut by operations and diminished by a hand,
leg, or lung, the 'I' remains the same — undiminished.

26. "Experience (of the Reality) is temporary or permanent.
The first experience is temporary and by concentration it
can become permanent. In the former the bondage is not
completely destroyed; it remains and asserts itself in due
course. But in the latter it is destroyed root and branch."

95

*Note*: This is of considerable significance to those who have
had an experience of the Self. In the first instance it
distinguishes between the temporary and the permanent
experience. Secondly it warns them that bondage will remain
round their necks and will cause their rebirth if they will
discontinue the practice. Bondage "asserts itself in due
course", if one is not careful to consolidate it into *sahaja*.
There must be no room for complacency.

27. "Seekers are of two classes: *kritopasaka* and *akritopasaka*. The former has already overcome his predispositions by steady devotion, so that his mind has become pure. He has some kind of experience <u>but does not comprehend it</u>. As soon as instructed by a competent Master, permanent experience results. The other class of seekers need great efforts to achieve this end." 95

*Note*: I have underlined "but does not comprehend it" to draw attention to the great importance of *sahaja* in the validation of the Realisation of the Self. Perfect firmness in the Being, and thus competence to teach it, is achieved only in *sahaja*, so that any knowledge about it before then cannot but be partial, even though the Self is being daily experienced in *samadhi*. Practice and the presence of the Master hasten the maturity of the *kritopasaka* for *sahaja*.

The other class of seekers, namely, the *akritopasaka*, the immature worshippers, have to slog their weary way uphill: they have to push, pull and heave to gain the stage of the *kritopasaka*, and then on to the Great Liberation.

28. "Of what nature is the realisation of Westerners who report flashes of Cosmic Consciousness?"
The Master answers: "It comes as a flash and disappears likewise in a flash. That which has a beginning must also end. Only when the ever-present consciousness is realised will it be permanent. Consciousness is indeed always with us. Everyone knows himself as 'I am'. No one can deny his own being." 96

*Note*: The answer to this question is fully given by the question itself. The reality that lasts not longer than a split second is as good as nothing. In the previous notes we have observed that even the daily experience of the pure consciousness in *nirvikalpa*, which lasts much longer than a mere flash, cannot give complete satisfaction and complete apprehension of all the ins and outs of the reality, but needs years of incessant practice — conscious and deliberate — to be perfected. That being the case, what value can be attached to these flashes? Moreover, who can tell whether they are of the genuine stuff, or mere gossamer tricks of the mind?

As for the "Cosmic Consciousness" itself, is there such consciousness at all in the sense of the Westerners? Bhagavan uses this term for Brahman, the Self, or *Chaitanya* (the pure consciousness); but to the Western "occultist" it has an altogether different flavour. Ours is the creed of the Absolute, wherein neither the individual nor the Cosmos exists; whereas the Western religious mystic and clairvoyant are dualists, who find great mysteries in the Cosmos and the individual, and still greater mysteries in the Cosmic Consciousness. Students of the Cosmic Consciousness have therefore to distinguish between the Advaitic meaning of it, and that of its Western counterpart. Probably this distinction has been in the mind of the questioner to impel him to enquire about "the nature of the realisation of Westerners", or else the realisation of the one consciousness is the same for all men without any distinction.

29.   "*Samadhi* transcends thought and speech and cannot be described. As the state of deep sleep cannot be described, more so is *samadhi*. You know that you are unconscious in deep sleep, but consciousness and unconsciousness are only modes of the mind. *Samadhi* transcends them. You know *samadhi* only when you are in *samadhi*."

110

*Note*: This is an answer to a request from an American lady to describe *samadhi*. It is obvious that no one can describe a thing which cannot be even thought of. Again, descriptions can be made in terms of sensuous experience — a perception, feeling or idea. But *samadhi* is neither an idea nor an object which is cognised in time and space in terms of shapes, colours, sounds, smells, etc. to be described. Being the pure mind itself, of which the questioner has not the remotest notion, description of it becomes impossible. Moreover, "you know what *samadhi* is only when you are in *samadhi*," when all thoughts have vanished and you are aware of nothing but the pure mind or consciousness — and not when you are out of it, at the time, for example, when the question is made. Thus the task of describing it becomes doubly difficult.

"You know that you are unconscious in deep sleep," does not mean that the knowledge of this unconsciousness, or the unconsciousness itself actually prevails in that state, but that it only appears as such to the person who is in the waking state. The unconsciousness of *sushupti* is not unconsciousness in *sushupti* itself. The man in *jagrat* judges things from his own state, which is that of the play of the senses and, therefore, of objectivity. When objectivity is absent, the state appears to him to be one of blank unconsciousness. Consciousness and unconsciousness mean nothing else to him but perception and non-perception of objects respectively, which is why the text speaks of them as "only modes of the mind". When viewed from inside the state of non-perception, that is, of *sushupti*, in this case, itself, consciousness is ever present as the man himself, who is at no time nonexistent. The state of *sushupti* is therefore not one of unconsciousness but of consciousness stripped of objective perceptions. In other words, *sushupti* is the state of the man himself, released from the infliction of body and senses, which disturb his peace in *jagrat*. It is the same as the state of *samadhi* with the difference that in the latter he is aware of himself as this pure consciousness. The *antahkarana*, or the aggregate psychical functions, including that of cognition, merge completely in this pure consciousness in *sushupti*, whereas in *samadhi* they are present but quiescent, inoperative.

> 30.  "The Heart is formless. Should we imagine it to have a shape and meditate on it?"
>
> Bhagavan: "No. Only the quest 'Who am I?' is necessary. Investigation of 'I' is the point, and not meditation on the Heart-centre. There is nothing like within and without. Both mean either the same thing or nothing.
>
> "Of course there is also the practice of meditation on the Heart-centre. But it is only a practice and not investigation. Only the one who meditates on the Heart can remain aware when the mind ceases to be active and remains still." 131

*Note*: It looks as though in the second half of this text Bhagavan retracts the statement in the first half not to meditate on the Heart centre. Actually he does not. Both statements are correct in their own contexts. In the first instance the question envisages the use of the imagination to give a form to the formless Heart, which is absurd. After all the Heart is naught but the Self, which is represented in our understanding by the principle 'I'. Would it not be therefore more logical and simpler to catch hold of this principle and enquire into it, rather than create an artificial image of it — the imageless — and meditate on it? This completely disposes of the question in the form it is put. (See texts 9 in Chapter X and 23 in this Chapter).

Now we turn to the positive side of the question, whether meditation on the Heart is possible. Bhagavan declares it to be possible, but not in the form of investigation, as it is done when the 'I' is the subject. Meditation on the Heart must be a special meditation, provided the meditator takes the Heart to be pure consciousness and has at least, an intuitive knowledge of what pure consciousness is. Only that meditation succeeds which has this intuitive knowledge, and is conducted with the greatest alertness, so that the moment thoughts cease, the mind perceives itself in its own home — the Heart itself. This is certainly more difficult to do than to investigate into the source of the 'I', because it is a direct assault on, rather direct contact with, the very source itself. It is no doubt the quickest method, but it exacts the greatest alertness and the most concentrated attention, denoting a greater *adhikara* (maturity).

31. "*Jnana* once revealed takes time to steady itself. The Self is certainly within the direct experience of every one, but not as one imagines it to be. It is only as it is. This experience is *samadhi*. Owing to the fluctuation of *vasanas*, *jnana* takes time to steady itself. Unsteady *jnana* is not enough to check rebirths. *Jnana* cannot remain unshaken side by side with *vasanas*. True that in the proximity of a great Master, the *vasanas* will cease to be active, the mind becomes still and *samadhi* results. Thus the disciple gains true knowledge and right experience in the presence of the Master. To remain unshaken in it further efforts are necessary. He will know it to be his real Being, and thus be liberated even while alive." 141

*Note*: This confirms text 26 in this chapter. Those who have experienced the Self and puzzle as to why they do not possess the Supreme Knowledge and Wisdom of Bhagavan are answered here. Bhagavan asks them to continue the practice to attain firmness in *jnana* and thus absolute perfection.

"Owing to the fluctuation of *vasanas*, *jnana* takes time to steady itself. . . . *Jnana* cannot remain unshaken side by side with *vasanas*." The senses are always active in the waking state even with the *Jnani*, and the habits of perception as well as the other peculiar mental habits continue to disturb the clear vision of the Self, if this is still of a tender age. The birth in the Self resembles the birth in this world of *jagrat*, which at first appears to the newborn incoherent and unintelligible, but gradually the day-to-day experience gives it significance and coherence. Infancy has to pass on to youth, then to adolescence, and finally to full adulthood. It is the same with the birth in the Self, but this process is quickened if the *sadhaka* remains with the Guru till the end. This is also a complete answer to those who believe that a short stay with the Master suffices for full-fledged *jnana*. Note 3 of the last chapter has already stressed the necessity of a long stay till *mukti* is attained.

"The Self is not as one imagines it to be. It is only as it is." This imagination of the Self is common to all. We imagine ourselves having height, breadth, colour, smell — a body, in short, — whereas in fact we are only 'I am', that is, the knower of the smell, of the colour, of the shape — the principle of knowledge, in effect. To know ourselves by direct experience as this principle, pure and simple, is *samadhi*. Protracted practice ripens into an intuitive approximation of the Self, otherwise the Self remains but an imaginary conception even for *sadhakas*.

32.    "Heart and *Sphurana* are the same as the Self. How can *Sphurana* be described? It includes all these (light, movement, etc.) — it is the Self. Fix your attention on it and do not let go the idea of its ultimate character."

160

*Note*: This is one more affirmation on Bhagavan's part of the identity of the *Sphurana* with the Self, or Heart. By "do not let go the idea of its ultimate character" he seems to advise concentration on the pure consciousness, which the meditator on the Heart has always to keep in mind and to which Bhagavan referred in text 30 above.

33. *"Be what you are.* There is nothing to come down or manifest itself. What is needed is losing the ego. That which is, is ever present. Even now you are It, and not apart from It. The blank is seen by you. You are always there. What do you wait for? The expectation to see and the desire to get something are all the working of the ego. You have fallen into the snare of the ego, which says all this. *Be yourself* and nothing more." 183

*Note*: This cannot be fully understood without its context. The questioner had asked the Guru of an Ashram that although he had kept his mind blank, as was required by the teaching of that Guru, awaiting God "to show Himself in His true Being" in it, he had so far experienced nothing, and the answer he had got from that Guru was to this effect: 'The attitude is right. The Power will come down from above. It is a direct experience.' Now he wants the opinion of Bhagavan on this. The above is Bhagavan's answer.

As we well see Bhagavan repudiates any such thing as descent of God, or of any Power. If you seek the reality, seek it here, for it is always abiding — it is here and now, fully manifested, or else it cannot be real. Reality that ascends and descends, that off and on absents itself is a dream. The test of reality is immutability, which implies eternal existence, eternal presence. That being the case, is God absent from here that appeal may be made to Him to come down? If He is, how would He be aware of our appeal? Secondly, does not this appeal expose our ignorance and the hollowness of our surrender? As for the powers of God, are they different from Him? Such notions are the creation of the imagination, the self-exaltation of the ego, Bhagavan asserts. Kill the ego and all these imaginations will cease: the Reality will stand revealed.

34. "It is enough if one surrenders oneself. Surrender is giving oneself up to the origin of one's being. Do not delude yourself by imagining such source to be some God outside you. One's source is within oneself. Give yourself up to it. That means that you should seek the source and merge in it. Because you imagine yourself to be out of it, you raise the question 'where is the source'?"

208

*Note*: This is a good way of defining surrender, and to many, a novel one. When we imagine our surrender to be to an outside God, here we are told that it is to no one but to the "origin of one's being", This delusion of an outside God Bhagavan knocks on the head by the firm reminder of "Do not delude yourself". He cannot be firmer than this.

The concept of an external Creator underlies the worship of almost all religions, which makes worshippers contract the habit of believing in a wrong external God, so that seekers on the path of *jnana* find themselves confronted with the necessity of extirpating this entrenched dogma, through the practice of *Vichara*, by turning their gaze inwardly towards the Self. Since there is nothing real beside the Self, the surrender of the external to the internal alone is true surrender: this is merging in the source of one's being.

Again, the answer to the question of "where the source of things is?" leads to oneself by a logical necessity. Being the originator of the question, one by sheer enquiry is pushed back to one's own source. From seeking it one ends by merging into it.

35. "Yes, control of mind and contemplation are interdependent. They must go on side by side. Practice

(*abhyasa*) and dispassion (*vairagya*) bring about the desired results by degrees. Dispassion checks the mind from going outward; practice keeps it turned inward. The two processes go on constantly within. Contemplation will in due course be successful."

220

*Note*: Efforts to meditate without the interference of thoughts which constantly harass the meditator is control; whereas contemplation is the meditation proper, that is, freedom from extraneous thoughts. Both processes have to go side by side naturally. But ability to control the mind does not come on a sudden, or from the first day or first month: constant practice is necessary, and this cannot be made except after one has sufficiently developed a dispassion for the things of the world.

It all begins with *viveka* — discrimination between real happiness and false happiness, between the really useful and the fictitiously useful. This advances to the renunciation of the fictitiously useful and aspiration for the really useful. Seeking the means of attaining the latter then begins, after which comes the practice of the means. This is *sadhana*, which ends in the complete success of the contemplation, right in Liberation itself.

36. "Grace is always there, but practice is necessary." 220

*Note*: In the chapter on Grace, Grace has been compared to Provident Fund which swells with the earnings — it is not a free gift. To expect Grace without earning it, is a thoughtless expectation. Moreover, there is no one to confer Grace: neither God, nor Guru, nor anyone. Grace confers itself. It is like an ocean which is ever full and ready to flow into all rivers and canals that have access to it, that have no

obstructions in its way. Exertion removes the obstructions
without the necessity of praying for it. If the sluicegate of a
canal, let us say, is closed, can any prayer help the water to
flow into the canal? Prayer for Grace helps to the extent that
it contains genuine *bhakti*, and if this increases to the point
of turning into a regular and continuous stream, it becomes
the practice of which Bhagavan speaks, which opens the
sluicegate and permits the flow of Grace in abundance.

> 37.  "Why does not the mind sink into the Heart even while
> meditating?"
>
> The Master answers: "A floating body does not readily
> sink unless some means are used for making it do so.
> Breath-control makes the mind quiescent. The mind
> must be alert and meditation pursued unremittingly
> even when it is at peace. Then it sinks into the Heart.
> Association with the wise also makes the mind sink into
> the Heart.
>
> "Such association is both mental and physical. The external
> Guru pushes the mind inward. The same Guru is also in
> the Heart of the seeker, and so he draws the latter's inward-
> bent mind into the Heart."                                   223

*Note*: We have had many occasions to discuss the supreme
value of the Guru's physical company and *Sat-sanga*. Here
we have another clear and precise statement from Bhagavan
himself on it — mentally and physically. The proximity of
the Guru is essential for rapid progress, and the more of it
the better. The evader cannot now so easily escape with his
specious plea to the contrary simply because it suits his
worldly purpose. The physical presence of the Master, to
repeat, is of the greatest help in this *sadhana*.

   "Why does not the mind sink into the Heart in
meditation?" Because concentration has not been sufficiently
heavy to "sink" it. The mind is, as we all know, restless by

nature, and has to be quietened by incessant practice. One of the methods, Bhagavan suggests, is breath-control, if a direct assault cannot be made on it by the mind itself through *vichara* and meditation. If you have not acquired mastery in marksmanship, your shots will be sure to go astray — they will never hit the target: but by repeated attempts they will.

38. "The mind does not now sink into the Heart because the latent tendencies stand as obstacles. They are removed by breath-control or association with the wise. In fact the mind is always in the Heart. But it is restive and moves about on account of latent tendencies. When the tendencies are made ineffective, it will be restful and at peace.
   "By breath-control the mind will be only temporarily quiescent, because the tendencies are still there. If the mind is transformed into the Self it will no longer give trouble. That is done by meditation." 223

*Note*: This develops the previous text and very rightly declares meditation to be superior to *pranayama*, or breath-control, in that the latter cannot destroy the *vasanas*, which are purely mental. Mental practices alone can destroy them through *vichara* and *dhyana*, which restore the mind to its pristine purity as the Self. How? Because the mind is itself the Self: "it is always in the Heart," nay, the Heart itself, but when thoughts or latent tendencies overwhelm it, they buoy it up to the surface, so to say, away from the reality of itself. That is why it strays into *ajnana*, it "floats". What *pranayama* does is simply to quieten its restlessness by the temporary suspension of the breath, but does not teach it the truth about its real nature, as does the *vichara*. Reflection reveals its relationship to the world on the one hand, and on the other to the reality that is itself. It shows it where the

obstruction to the vision of its true self lies, and how it can
be removed, and *dhyana* actually removes the obstruction by
stopping all thoughts and all *vasanas*. *Vichara* and *dhyana* are
the reverse and obverse of the Advaitic *sadhana*, whereas
*pranayama* is a simple mechanical device — in this line a mere
crutch, for when Bhagavan suggests *pranayama* it is always
on the understanding that it is combined with *dhyana*, which
follows it up after it (*pranayama*) has temporarily subdued
the waves of the mind. Let us remember again that the transformation of the mind into the Self is effected through *dhyana*
alone or the right *japa*, which is as good as *dhyana*.

> 39. "There is no entity by the name mind. Because of the
> emergence of thoughts we surmise a thing from which
> they start. That we term mind. When we probe to see
> what it is, there is nothing like it. *Buddhi* or intellect is
> the thinking or discriminating faculty. But these are mere
> names. Ego, mind and intellect are all the same. Whose
> mind? Whose intellect? The ego's. Is the ego real? No.
> We confound the ego and call it intellect or mind."
>
> 237

*Note*: Philosophers, metaphysicians, and theologians will open
their eyes wide at this statement of Bhagavan. How they
wrangle about words which mean absolutely nothing! *Buddhi,
manas, ahankar, chitta*, etc., seem to them to be watertight
psychical compartments, with well-defined boundaries and
so on; whereas in fact they are only the creation of the analytical
mind. They create the compartments and then get confused
and confounded by them. All these are but different functions
of the mind or the Self, outside of which they have no existence
whatsoever. They should be totally ignored in our search for
truth. Our aim is the pure mind itself, *not its functions* — not
its manifestations as phenomena, as perceptions, as sensations,

as ideas, as imagination. All these are irrelevant to our search, and so we have to discard them in order to arrive at the pure mind which emits, or secretes them, as it were. As long as our attention is fixed on them, we can never reach their substratum, the Real. They are nothing but shadows, and thus, as Bhagavan says, unreal, "mere names." "When we probe" into them they all disappear. The irony of it is that all the sciences known to man, from physics down to psychology, and even philosophy itself, deal with only these unreal psychical processes, *never with the mind* itself.

40. "To realise the Self effort is necessary. Just as water is got by boring wells, so also you realise the Self by investigation."                                           240

*Note*: As we have already observed, efforts are absolutely indispensable, with due respect to the modern prophets of effortlessness. Efforts are made to reach the effortless state which is unalloyed bliss and eternal.

41. "*Ravi marga* (the Path of the Sun) is *jnana*. Moon *marga* is yoga. They think after purifying the 72,000 *nadis* in the body, *sushumna* is entered and the mind passes up to the *sahasrara* and there is nectar trickling. These are all mental concepts of the man who is already overwhelmed by the world concepts. Other concepts are now added in the shape of this yoga. The objects of all these is to rid the man of concepts and to make him inhere in the pure Self, i.e. in the absolute consciousness, which is free from thoughts. Why not go straight to it? Why add new encumbrances to the already existing ones?"

251-52

*Note*: The Path of the Sun is the *vichara* and *dhyana*, which rid one of all concepts and all thoughts, so that the pure consciousness may be perceived. "The Path of the Moon" is indirect and leads not to the Heart but to the head. The latter passes through the *sushumna* where the breath is ultimately confined through the practice of *pranayama*, and thence to the *sahasrara* (brain centre), where bliss, or nectar is said to be stored up. Bhagavan avers that the Moon Path is based on mere conjectures, "concepts," which have been magnified and diversified in all sorts of ways to make it appear difficult and mysterious, particularly by the *Hatha* Yogis and *Kundalini* Yogis. "Clairvoyants" go even farther and write special books on the *Chakras* — their shapes, their colours, their movements, the special *siddhis* they confer. Yet all these are of no use in the search for the reality, which has neither shape nor colour and is certainly devoid of mysteries. Except the seekers of *siddhis* the professed aim of all these systems of Yoga is the reality. That being the case, Bhagavan asks, then why all these devious routes? Why add new notions to the millions with which we are already saddled and of which yogis have to rid themselves? Why not go straight by the "Path of the Sun" and save much time and trouble?

42.  "*Kevala nirvikalpa* takes place even in the *tanumanasi* stage....
      The three classes of *jnanis*, namely, the dull, middling and
      superior are due to their *prarabdha*, according as it is strong,
      middling and weak respectively. There is no difference in
      their *samadhi* or their *jnana*. The classification is only from
      the standpoint of the observer. The seventh and highest
      stage is that of the *Turiyaga* which is beyond words.
      "There is no need to discuss these points. *Jivanmukti*
      and *Videhamukti* are differently described by different
      authorities. *Videhamukti* is also said to occur even to *jnanis*
      who are still in a body."                                    256

*Note*: This text is of special interest to those who are very near the end of their spiritual journey. It encourages them to quicken their step that they may have a taste of *nirvikalpa*. which Bhagavan says, can be experienced even in a tenuous state of the mind, before all the *vrittis* and *vasanas* have been completely destroyed, a taste which will consolidate their faith in the glorious destiny which is soon to be fulfilled.

These three divisions of the *jnanis* must not be taken too seriously, for they mean nothing to the *jnanis* themselves. The *Jnani*, whether he is of the first, second, or third class, has attained Liberation from the wheel of birth and death, and does not care a straw how he and his attainments appear to others. The third degree *Jnani's prarabdha* is still "strong" on him, that is, on his worldly circumstances, and may not cause him even to be recognised as a *Jnani*. It is not "strong" in his own perception, but in the treatment of him by others in this respect. Those who have lived with our Master Sri Ramana Maharshi, who is taken to be the very highest, the *Turiyaga*, cannot be impressed by anyone lesser than he. Him alone they call *Jnani* and would ignore any claim of *jnana* on behalf of another. They pitch their mark so high because of the sublimity of their Master's attainments that the three classes of *Jnanis* mentioned above pass them unnoticed. This does not mean that these *Jnanis* do not exist. In fact they do, and live their normal life unconcerned with what others think of them. Some may have a large number of followers, and some may have none at all. A few may not even like to be recognised as *Jnanis* to spare themselves the inconvenience of taking disciples, preferring to remain in obscurity to enjoy their individual freedom. The recognition, however, depends upon the individual *prarabdha*, which affects only the *Jnani's* external circumstances, as it has been already said, and not the internal, which is the same for all *Jnanis* and all their classes and divisions.

On the contrary there may be some people, who have developed a highly intuitive intellect and who, without being *Jnanis*, shine out as great teachers with tremendous following, attracted by one trait of their intellectual or aesthetic abilities or other. Popularity and considerable reputation are thus not at all a criterion by which the *Jnani* and his spiritual greatness should be appraised. *Prarabdha* is responsible for all this worldly show.

As for *Jivanmukti* and *Videhamukti*, these are terms which usually indicate the states of the living *Jnani* and the one who has discarded his physical body respectively. *Videha* means without a body, so *videhamukti* means the state of the liberated man who is bodiless. But the same term also applies to even the *Jivanmukta*, because, as far as his own perception of himself goes, he is bodiless, being the pure Brahman, the Pure Consciousness, though he is still in a body. That is why Bhagavan avoids talking about this distinction, which is really nonexistent at his own level (See text 56).

43.    "When thoughts cross the mind and effort is made to eliminate them, the effort is termed meditation. Meditation is only negative inasmuch as thoughts are kept away." 294

*Note*: Warding off thoughts is one of the negative functions of meditation. Text 35 speaks of control and contemplation as if they were separate processes. They are no more separate from each other than chewing is from eating. Control, concentration, contemplation, meditation are parts of the one and the same process, which goes by the general name of *dhyana*, which in the last analysis proves to be a negative process. The positive side of the practice is its aim, which is *Atmanishtha*, fixation in the Self. The latter cannot be achieved without the former, which clears the decks for it. Unless thoughts and feelings are swept away, the stable consciousness from which they rise and which underlies them cannot be perceived. In fact even in the investigation there is nothing positive because it is only a process of elimination, not of acquisition. The ego and all the *upadhis* have to be liquidated for the reality to show itself from underneath them. As the ever-shining sun cannot be seen when it is covered by thick clouds, so is the pure consciousness hidden from perception by these accretions and superimpositions.

44. "Meditation is sticking to one thought. That single thought keeps away other thoughts; distraction of mind is a sign of its weakness. By constant meditation it gains strength, i.e., weakness of fugitive thoughts gives place to the enduring background free from thoughts. This expanse devoid of thoughts is the Self. Mind in purity is the Self."

293

*Note*: The previous text defines meditation as the effort to eliminate thoughts, and this one as sticking to one thought. Both definitions on examination prove to be the same. To stop all thoughts one thought should be chosen to tie the mind with. This will automatically exclude all other thoughts; for there is no such thing as mind absolutely free from thoughts in *jagrat*. The aim is to restrain the distractions which weaken it. Practice reduces the distractions — the mental waves — and thus strengthens the mind, till absolute mental stability is gained, which is not other than the Self, for stable — waveless — mind is the pure mind, the pure Consciousness. This is simple to understand, Bhagavan often tells us, and easy to practice.

45. "Trance is the natural state. Although there are activities and phenomena, yet they do not affect the trance. If these are realised to be not apart from the Self, the Self is realised. It is to be realised with the mind. The Pure Mind, that

is, the mind free from thoughts is the Self. The pure
mind is beyond the impure mind."                    317

*Note*: The word Bhagavan uses is *samadhi* and not trance,
which is the traditional translation of *samadhi*, and which the
recorder of this "Journal" has adopted. This translation is,
of course, not only inapt but defective. If we retain the word
*samadhi* even in English, there will be less trouble for the
reader to follow the idea.

In this text Bhagavan removes much of the misappre-
hensions which hover round the term *samadhi* and restores
it to its natural significance as being the natural state of all
things. Trance, far from conveying this idea, wraps it up in
dark clouds and darker associations. It can now be observed
how faulty translations of key words are dangerous.

In *Sahaja samadhi*, the permanent state of the *Jnani*, as
of Bhagavan himself, the world does not disappear, as it does
in *kevala nirvikalpa*, but it is all there — with its shape and
colours, smells, tastes and sounds; with its solids and liquids,
summers, springs and autumns; with its cinemas and music
halls — all its fun and frolics, all its tragedies and comedies
— wholly and vividly the same. But these no longer stand as
isolated or connected islands in an external boundless space;
no longer as God's creation; no longer as the rainbow beauties
that had once enthralled his young imagination and
dominated his youthful heart. They are now mere thoughts
and sensations, mere wisps of his *jagrat* dreams, in which he,
the dreamer, alone is real. They no longer cloud the
perception of his own reality. In another sense they are also
real, because he, the perceiver, is real. They are "the stuff of
which dreams are made", and dreams rise only from the
dreamer, who is their soul and substance: as the substance is
real, so they must be.

Here again Bhagavan identifies the pure mind with the Self. Mind is therefore not *manas* — another wrong translation by the old scholars which has become traditional, sacrosanct in their eyes, and which we repudiate. Mind is mind. When it is covered by thoughts it is called *manas* or impure mind. When thoughts are arrested it is the pure mind or Self.

46.   "The Bible says, 'Be still and know that I am God.' Stillness is the sole requisite for the realisation of the Self as God. The whole Vedanta is contained in the two Biblical statements: 'I AM THAT I AM', and 'BE STILL AND KNOW THAT I AM GOD'."      338

*Note*: The questioner is an American lady who thinks that the affirmation of 'I am the Supreme Being' should be more helpful than the quest 'Who am I?' The former, in her opinion, is a positive, whereas the latter a negative, or neutral, approach. It is obvious that she has completely missed the point of the quest. The quest is an investigation, not self-hypnosis, nor Couéism, which flourishes on "positive" auto-suggestions. Bhagavan had answered that she should first find out who is the one who affirms before she starts affirming, which would compel her to enquire into the nature of the empirical 'I', the 'I' which she thinks herself to be, and which has, at first sight, nothing of the "Supreme" in it.

In any case to arrive at the Being of her suggestion the mind must be still, hence Bhagavan twice quotes the Old Testament to explain his meaning to her. The first, namely, 'I am that I am,' conveys the nature of the reality, as the Being, or, as she calls it the Supreme Being; and the second, namely, 'Be still and know that I am God,' the method of attaining It. These two dicta, Bhagavan opines, express the heart and essence of the Vedanta — its Goal and Path at once.

47.  "While not actively conscious of any kind of selfhood, there is a deep quietness in the mind. Is one at such times ready to dive into the Self? Or is this condition unhealthy, a sort of self-hypnotism?

Bhagavan: "There is consciousness along with the quietness in the mind: this is exactly the state to be aimed at. The fact that there is a doubt on this point shows that the state is not steady but casual.

"When deep quietness prevails without obstructing the consciousness, where is the need to dive?"          348

*Note*: The experience of the questioner is interesting, inasmuch as it is precursory to the great experience of the Self. He is then just below the mental waves, and is feeling his way to the substratum. He asks if he should then "dive", and Bhagavan answers that there is no need to do so, for the consciousness which is aware of the quiet is the reality itself, which means that the questioner has only to be aware of that consciousness.

We have often observed that consciousness prevails at all times, for through it we are conscious of things. To catch consciousness by itself, all we have to do is to drop the things, which our friend the questioner seems to have done, as is evidenced by the feeling of inner peace, which the thoughts, or things of the mind, would not have otherwise permitted. All he has now to do is to try to be aware of the consciousness that feels, or notices, the quiet, which is already present and does not need to be dived for to be cognised. A little shrewdness, so to say, a little more alertness at that supreme moment will be sure to do the trick.

48.  "Just as by churning the curd, butter is extracted and by friction, fire is kindled, even so by unswerving vigilant constancy in the Self, ceaseless like the unbroken filamentary flow of oil is generated the natural or changeless

*nirvikalpa samadhi*, which spontaneously yields that direct perception of Brahman, which is at once Knowledge and Experience and which transcends time and space. This is Self-realisation, cutting asunder the *Hridaya-granthi*, or the knot of the Heart which is constituted of delusions, of ignorance, of the vicious and age-long tendencies of the mind. All doubts are thus dispelled and the bondage of karma is severed."     349

*Note*: The churning of the curd and friction refer to the ceaseless churning of the enquiry. The "unswerving vigilant constancy in the Self" is the holding on to the *dhyanic* current which resembles the unbroken flow of oil — vigilant because it is sufficiently alert to ward off digressions as well as sleep. This last inclination is as troublesome as the inclination to reminisce. Success in this leads to *nirvikalpa*, wherein the knot of ignorance which is lodged in the Heart of the *jiva* snaps, opening wide the door of Self-realisation, which is usually barred by this "*Hridaya-granthi*".

Let it not be supposed that in *samadhi* thoughts stop like a snuffed out candle; for that is not at all possible. Highly tenuous thoughts continue to hover all the time, and the alertness continues to be exercised against them at the same time; yet peace supreme reigns, and the Self is clearly experienced. The presence of thoughts in their subtlest form is due to the presence of the senses in their quiescent state. The senses — strictly speaking, the *antahkarana* (all the processes of thought) — merge in the Self only in sleep and in *videhamukti:* they do not merge in *samadhi*, or otherwise *samadhi* would be nothing but sleep, wherefrom nothing could be brought back to the waking state, and the Self would remain ever unknown. It is only because the *antahkarana* is present in *samadhi*, though quiescent — or because quiescent — that the Self is cognised and we have all the *Srutis, Smritis* and everything that is known about the Self. To this presence the Rishis owe their *jnana* and Liberation. In *sushupti* there is no cognition of the Self, because the faculty of cognition is not present but has merged in the Self, like all the other faculties.

49.   "The Shastras say that we must serve the Guru for twelve years for getting Self-realisation. What can the Guru do? Can he hand it over to the disciple? Is not the Self always realised? Confusing the body with the Self is due to ignorance. If ignorance is wiped out the confusion will end and true knowledge unfolded. By remaining in contact with realised sages one gradually loses his ignorance till it disappears totally. The eternal Self is thus revealed.

"Without understanding it aright people think that the Guru teaches something like "TATVAMASI" and immediately the disciple realises "I am Brahman". In their ignorance they conceive Brahman to be something much bigger and far more powerful than anything else. With a limited 'I' man is so stuck up and wild. What will he be if the same 'I' increased enormously? He will certainly be proportionately more ignorant and more foolish. This false 'I' must perish. Its annihilation is the fruit of service to the Guru. Realisation is eternal and is not granted by the Guru. The Guru helps only the removal of ignorance — that is all."                                      350

*Note*: Bhagavan is certainly frank in his attitude towards orthodoxy and the way people interpret the *Shastras*. In ancient days, as we read in the *Mahabharata* and elsewhere, lack of accuracy was winked at and calculation of periods very loose. The year particularly was not the same as our year, nor were the numerals of the same values as their present namesakes, so that when we read of a certain Rishi having remained in meditation or *samadhi* for a thousand or a million years, we will be highly foolish if we take the figures or the years in their dictionary meanings. Moreover, hyperboles were the very salt of their poetic effusions. When they tell us, for example, that it is easier for a person to bring down the sun for one's child to play with than to get at *Paramatman*, the Supreme Self, we should know how to take it. Thousands upon thousands of seekers have so far passed through the portals of *Mukti*, but not one has succeeded to bring down the sun to play ball with. We are not to take literally all what we read in the *Shastras:* gold and dross are mixed together in them, either by accident or design to make the strong-minded pick up the valuable gold, leaving the dross to the weak ones who need them.

Now the twelve-year service to the Guru as the price of *Mukti* is patently absurd. For not all servers are of the same degree of purity, nor of the same preparations, nor of the same surrender-attitude, nor of the same spiritual culture. How can all succeed in passing the winning-post at one and the same time, at the tick of the twelfth year? Secondly is *Mukti* a thing which is in the hands of the Guru to grant or withhold? The Self being ourselves, is it the gift of the external Guru that we are now in existence, that we are what we are and where we are? If not, how are we entitled to presume that the Guru is the dispenser of the reality to his disciples? All he can do is to help them perceiving it. We are that reality, but, owing to the *upadhis* which are superimposed on us, we are unable to perceive ourselves as in truth we are. The Guru gives us a helping hand, which is all he can do.

If the twelve-year service means anything, it is to convey the idea of constancy of residence with the Guru.

Again, the conception of a tremendous Brahman variously described by various pseudo Self-realised teachers precludes even veteran *sadhakas* from recognising the Brahman in themselves or in those who have actually realised it; more so those who take literally what they read in various scriptures about a personal Creator, who is full of actions and qualities and has infinite powers. If the idea that one day they will be that Almighty God is allowed to go to their puny heads, they will have any amount of trouble for their sins, and Bhagavan's delightful tirade will be a good and timely warning. "With a limited 'I'," he cautions, "man is so stuck up and wild. What will he be if the same 'I' increases enormously? This false 'I' must perish."

50.  "How to meditate? Concentrate on that God or *mantra* which you like best. If a single thought prevails, all other thoughts are put off and finally eradicated. *Dhyana* is a fight. As soon as you begin meditation other thoughts will join together and try to sink the single thought to which you try to hold. The good thought will gradually gain strength through practice, and will put other thoughts to flight. This is the battle royal constantly taking place in meditation.
     "One wants to rid oneself of misery for which he requires peace of mind. Peace of mind, which means the clearing of the mind from all thoughts, is brought about by *dhyana*."
                                                                        371

*Note*: We meditate with the ultimate object of acquiring peace. For the mind has the tendency of forming vortices of thoughts about one object or another, one problem or another, round which it circles ceaselessly. We thus live in whirlpools of constant worries, at one time patent, at another time subdued, from which we find no escape except in meditation or mind control.

The single thought which Bhagavan recommends us to take up for meditation acts both as a calming influence and as an anchor to tie up the mind to, to the exclusion of all other thoughts, including those which cause the worries. This thought may be chosen *ad libitum* from among the Gods, the *mantras*, the teachers, or from some lofty ideals, or even virtues, for which the meditator has a special partiality.

At first the meditator will be astounded to find new thoughts swarming up in his mind as soon as the latter has succeeded to a degree of ridding itself from the surface waves which had been disturbing it. These are memories of the experiences through which he had passed in life: they specifically choose moments of attenuated mind to escape from the confinement of the subconscious, into which they have been stored up from a very early age, and come into prominence to divert the meditator's attention to them. Extreme alertness on the latter's part has thus to be exercised at every step in the meditation to oppose their intrusion. This "battle royal" is finally won through perseverance in the practice.

> 51. "When *dhyana* is well-established it cannot be given up. It will go on automatically even when you are engaged in work, play or enjoyment. It will persist in sleep too. *Dhyana* must become so deep-rooted that it will be natural to one."
>
> 371

*Note*: When *dhyana* has taken a firm grip on the mind it establishes a *dhyanic* current, which is ceaselessly directed towards the Heart, like the magnetic needle which perennially points to the magnetic Pole, irrespective of one's preoccupations with other matters.

By its "persisting in sleep" it is not meant that meditation is then practised deliberately and in one's full awareness, but that the flow of the *dhyanic* current persists as impressions in the same way as the impressions of *jagrat* experience are carried over to the dream state, whether one is aware of it or not. It has been the experience of some *sadhakas* that after the first experience of the Self in *samadhi*, and before they have attained firmness in it, they mechanically attempt to capture, and sometimes do capture, the *samadhi* state in the dream also. But once a substantial degree of firmness is achieved in *jagrat*, such dreams no longer recur, except extremely seldom; for one has by then established oneself almost permanently in the reality which prevails in the waking, dreaming and dreamless sleep.

52. "The difference between the external and the internal *nirvikalpa* is this: the former is holding to the reality while witnessing the world, without reacting to it from within. There is the stillness of a waveless ocean. The internal *nirvikalpa* involves loss of body-consciousness."

406

*Note*: In *samadhi* the Self is witnessed in all its purity, and there is profound peace. As we have already studied in *Note 48*, the world as most tenuous thoughts, like gossamer cloud that hangs about the orb of the sun at midday, continue to hang about, but without dimming the perception of the Self.

"The stillness of a waveless ocean" is at once graphic and picturesque. This still vastness is the empirical space with which we are familiar, but which is actually the ether of the Heart, into which all the things live, move and have their being.

The internal *nirvikalpa*, the *Kevala*, wipes out all thoughts, including that of the body. This does not mean loss of consciousness, as in sleep, for that will no longer be *samadhi*, but *sushupti*. *Samadhi* must be in *jagrat* — let us hold this idea tight, and never forget it. The various accounts we read in books about *nirvikalpa*, particularly by modern writers, are in the main based on imagination. Some followers of *Kundalini* yoga allow themselves to be carried away by the *kevala kumbhaka* and get trapped into *laya*, a state resembling deep sleep, which they mistake for *nirvikalpa*, although they remain unaware of the Self, the basic requisite of *samadhi*. (*Vide* Appendix.)

Therefore by loss of body-consciousness Bhagavan does not mean swoon or *laya*, but loss of the body-idea, or body-thought, which vaguely prevails in the external *nirvikalpa*. Total loss of body and world consciousness, as in sleep, never takes place in any *samadhi*, at all events not in that of the *dhyana* yoga, for then the Self would no longer be cognised, which is a necessary condition in the true *samadhi*. *Samadhi*, I wish again to emphasise, is dwelling in the Self in the waking state, that is, when the senses are all out but quiescent — rather rendered quiescent by meditation, — and never when the senses are merged in the Self and the world is totally extinguished, as it happens in deep sleep. We must also not forget that it is the *jagrat* mind that seeks and makes efforts to attain the Reality, and that it is, therefore, in *jagrat* that it has to be satisfied.

53.  "You say that the mind is like a cork and does not sink. What does it matter if the mind is active? It is so only on the substratum of the Self. Hold to the Self even during mental activities."                                                  406

*Note*: This requires some explanation, for it is likely to mislead new students. We have been repeatedly told that the substratum cannot be witnessed so long as it is covered by mental activities, and in this text Bhagavan says just the reverse, namely, that it would not matter if the activities were present. The text here speaks to the person who has experienced the Self but has not yet made it *sahaja*. For such an one mental activities no longer obstruct the Self, for he has already experienced them as superimpositions on it, so that he has only to hold to the Self always at the same time as witnessing the activities much like remembering the canvas while enjoying the sight of the pictures painted on it. When this practice is perfected, it is then called *sahaja samadhi*, and the *sadhaka* a full-fledged *Jnani* or *Jivanmukta*.

54. "*Vritti Jnana* alone can destroy *ajnana*. Absolute *jnana* is not inimical to *ajnana*."                                    629

*Note*: Merely being in the Self in *kevala nirvikalpa* does not dispel ignorance, although it brings Liberation from birth and death if turned into *Sahaja*. It is investigation into the nature of the Self and the world, and relating the one to the other in what is called as argumentative meditation or *Vichara*, that results in the knowledge which destroys ignorance. Absolute *jnana* or complete merging of the *jiva* into the absolute Consciousness in *Turyatita* is devoid of all mental modification (*vritti*) to learn anything during meditation to destroy ignorance: even the awareness 'I am this' is absent at the moment. Bhagavan calls this *Swarupa Jnana* (Knowledge of one's very Self — in its purest state) and can also be gained through *Vritti Jnana*.

It must not be assumed that all yogis attain *jnana* through *vichara*, as Bhagavan did, yet they are not precluded from being *Jivanmuktas* of the highest order.

55. "Deep sleep is nothing but the experience of pure being."
617

*Note*: The word 'experience' here may give the impression that the sleeper is aware of his being in dreamless sleep. In fact he is not, since all the faculties of cognition are then withdrawn into him. In both dreamless sleep and *videhamukti* no cognition of the being is possible, which is the reason the *Bhagavata* gives for taking a body by the Self and becoming a *jiva*, so that with the manifestation of the *antahkarana* (inner organ) — *manas, buddhi, ahankara* and *chitta* (the thinking faculty, intellect, ego and memory) — through the body the *jiva* may perceive himself as he is by nature, as the pure *chit* and enjoy the bliss of this realisation.

56. "There are five states for the individual. They are *jagrat, svapna, sushupti, Turiya* and *Turyatita*. . . If in *jagrat* the Heart is not relinquished, the mental activities are still and Brahman alone is contemplated, the state is called *Turyatita*. Again when the individual merges in the supreme the state is called *Turyatita*... The clear-sighted yogi abides only in *Turiya* and the highest yogi remains in *Turyatita* alone." 617

*Note*: Although many Upanishads do not speak of *Turyatita* (beyond the Fourth), as, for example, the *Mandukya*, which deals only with the first four states, experience and a number of minor Upanishads prove its existence as a state deeper than *Turiya* (the Fourth). Yet *Turiya* alone is sufficient to secure *sahaja* and Liberation, which is all that the yogi aims at achieving. Long abidance in *Turiya* culminates in the experience of *Turyatita*, which is total merging of the individual in the Supreme Being (*Brahman*). Here the *Jivanmukta* is actually a *videhamukta*, that is, while in life he dwells in, and is aware of, the very state in which he will be after shedding the body. This is the highest that is possible for any *jiva* to attain.

# CHAPTER FOURTEEN

# THE JNANI OR JIVANMUKTA

1.   "A child and a *Jnani* are similar in a way. The interest of
     the child in things ends with the things. These leave no
     impressions in the child's mind. The same is the case
     with the *Jnani*."                                      9

*Note*: Desires are the cause of all our trouble. We look around
this magnificent world of diversity and desire the things
which impress us most, and so do our best to obtain them.
We sacrifice a lot and suffer any amount of inconvenience
for the sake of the desired object till we get it. Yet our trouble
does not end with this acquisition, for new aims and objects
rise before us and lure us into new desires and what we call
new needs, for which we have again to exert and again to
suffer; and so on and on endlessly. Thus we remain bound
hand and foot to the world without rest and without
satisfaction. But the *Jnani*, having cultivated and achieved
desirelessness, has not the least interest in the world around
him, so that his perceptions do not leave any impression on
his mind. Even if he evinces an interest in an object it is only
one of curiosity, much like that of a child in its surroundings,
which passes away the moment it turns its back on them.

2.   "The look of the *Jnani* has a purifying effect. Purification
     cannot be visualised. Just as a piece of coal takes long to
     be ignited, a piece of charcoal takes a short time, and a

mass of gunpowder is instantaneously ignited, so it is
with grades of men coming in contact with *Mahatmas*."
155

*Note*: This is an answer to a question by an English disciple
— one of the earliest — who has been staying in the Ashram
for three months and has yet been unaware of any spiritual
benefit to himself from it. The 'grade' of the disciple in
question need not be inferred from this question or this
answer; for Bhagavan assures us that the process and degree
of purification cannot be assessed easily: it goes its own quiet
way without the direct knowledge of the disciple concerned
or of anyone else. This has been the experience of almost
each and everyone in this Ashram. Even on the very thres-
hold of the Supreme Experience one is likely to be almost
unaware of its imminence. It is small wonder therefore that
this disciple's surface consciousness was not aware of what
was going on in its depths. The purification incessantly goes
on in the presence of the Master, irrespective of the degree
of impurity which the disciple brings with him. The
difference in time of attaining *jnana* between one disciple
and another naturally lies in the difference in the degrees
of impurity which they respectively bring with them.

3.  "Is Maharshi's teaching the same as Shankara's?" The
    Master answers about himself: "Maharshi's teaching is
    only an expression of his own experience and realisation.
    Others find that it tallies with Sri Shankara's. A realised
    man uses his own language." 189

*Note*: This is an autobiographical answer, which may be
applicable to most *Jnanis*. The peculiarities of Bhagavan's
Realisation consist in the unique fact that Realisation came
to him when he was still in the prime of life and had not yet

had any contact with philosophical or metaphysical elements, either through reading or through human guidance. He had been preoccupied with his studies for the Matriculation Examination, when the Realisation knocked him down and clean out of his studies. The result was that when later he recounted his experiences in the ordinary language, the learned among the listeners found them to be identical with Shankara's philosophy.

4.  "A Self-realised being cannot help benefiting the world His very existence is the highest good."         210

*Note*: This should satisfy those who criticise the *Jnani* as a useless ascetic, should they be fortunate enough to read it. The wisdom that flows from his lips and the purity of his life and conduct stand as shining ideals for humanity to emulate, or aspire for, which no amount of preaching Socialism, Communism and philanthropy can do. What has all this preaching created except more antagonism, more divisions, more jealousy, and thus more hatred in the world. If these preachers really mean well and are sincere, they should turn into true ascetics and become Saints themselves and see the difference between their old preaching and the good they can do with their holiness and purity by their mere presence. If they cannot do that, they should mind their own business, and try to bring peace and good to themselves before they can stand before the world and boast of doing good to others. See text 7 below.

5.  Speaking of *Jnanis* who depart from the world without leaving a body behind, like Manickavasagar, Bhagavan said: "The gross body is only the concrete form of the subtle stuff — the mind. When the mind melts away and blazes forth as light, the body is consumed in that

process. Nandanar is another whose body disappeared in blazing light."

An English disciple pointed out the case of Biblical Elijah whose body disappeared in the same way and wanted to know if Christ's body did the same. The Master replied: "No. Christ's body was left as a corpse, which was at first entombed, whereas the others did not leave corpses behind." 215

*Note*: This text should be studied in the light of Bhagavan's general Advaitic teachings.

"When the mind melts away and blazes forth as light, the body is consumed in that process," is the rationale of the disappearance of the body of the *Siddha Jnani* at his *Mahasamadhi* — so-called death. This helps us to understand the relation of the mind to the body on the one hand and to the light to which the quoted sentence refers on the other. But first we have to observe that the disintegration of the body takes place only through a process of which some *Jnanis* known as *Siddhas* — not all *Jnanis*, — whose *prarabdha* entitles them to it, have the 'Key'. The benefits of such 'miraculous' performances by some *Siddhas* consist of creating tremendous psychological effects on the common people, increasing their faith. But most *Jnanis* do not approve of them, because, while they increase the people's devotion, they tend to encourage credulity, superstitions, witchcraft and magic, which they are out to combat by teaching the Truth, the whole Truth, and nothing but the Truth.

6. "Is there no 'I-am-the-body' idea for the *Jnani*? If, for instance, Sri Bhagavan is bitten by an insect, is there no sensation?"

Bhagavan: "There is the sensation and there is also the 'I-am-the-body' idea. The latter is common to both the *Jnani* and the *ajnani* with this difference, that the *ajnani* thinks 'only the body is myself', whereas the *Jnani* knows 'all this is the Self', or 'all this is Brahman; if there be pain, let it be. It is also part of the Self. The Self is perfect'.

"Now with regards to the actions of the *Jnanis*, they are only so-called because they are ineffective. Generally the actions get embedded as *samskaras* (impressions) in the individual. That can be only so long as the mind is fertile, as is the case of the *ajnani*. With a *Jnani* the mind is only surmised; he has already transcended the mind. Because of his apparent activity the mind has to be inferred in his case, and that mind is not fertile like that of an *ajnani*. Hence it is said that the *Jnani's* mind is Brahman. Brahman is certainly no other than the *Jnani's* mind. *Vasanas* cannot bear fruit in that soil. His mind is barren, free from the *vasanas*, etc.

"However, since *prarabdha* is conceded in his case, *vasanas* also must be supposed to exist. But they are only *vasanas* for enjoyment, leaving no impressions to be the seeds for future *karma*."    383

*Note*: In this text we have a full view of the *Jnani's* state: in pains, in action, in the working out of an old, and the generation of a new, karma, etc. It all amounts to this: his perceptions of pain and pleasure and of the world are exactly like those of the *ajnani*, as we have discussed in Note 45 of the last chapter. He sees other bodies and his own exactly as others see them, but, unlike others, he knows the truth about them. A peasant who, for the first time goes to a cinema-show and sees fierce fire raging on the screen, starts screaming and tries to run out of the theatre, taking the fire to be real; whereas the others sit back in their chairs unconcerned. This is the exact difference between the *Jnani* and the *ajnani* in their perceptions. Both see the very same sights, yet their knowledge of them vastly differs.

As for the actions of the *Jnani* they are equally productive — often even more so — as those of the *ajnani* (the word 'ineffective' in the text is likely to be misinterpreted as qualifying actions, whereas it qualifies the production of *samskaras*), but they are without *vasanas*, although they appear as if they were. They resemble Coleridge's wonderful pen-picture of "a painted ship on a painted ocean", though ship and ocean are real. The actual ship is there, the actual ocean is also there, but there is no movement in either on account of the curse. The same are the *vasanas* of the *Jnani* which leave no impressions on his mind. The driving force in an action which produces Karma is its motive, which is absent in the *Jnani's*; hence there is no creation of a new karma for him. The actor is there, the action is also there, but the driving force of the action is, in his case, automatic, being impersonal, *vasana*-less. The *Srutis* compare it to the fried seed which can no longer sprout. That is why the action of the *Jnani* is viewed as inaction. The *Jnani* appears to act, and efficiently too, but he is not acting at all. This is the significance of inaction in action and action in inaction. The motiveless mind is Brahman Itself. This is one of the most revealing statements of Bhagavan.

7. "The Sage is characterised by eternal and intense activity. His stillness is like the apparent stillness of a fast-rotating top. Its very speed cannot be followed by the eye, and so it appears to be still. So is the apparent inaction of the Sage. This must be explained because the people generally mistake his stillness to be inertness. It is not so." 599

*Note*: Bhagavan has reasons to explain this truth about the *Jnani* to the critics of his "inactive" life. There is no activity under the sun which is more intense than that of the *Jnani*, because he is the plenum, the pure *chaitanya* which is the storehouse of all the energy in the universe. Thus the critics will do well to reflect before they pass a sentence on the *Jnani's* activity or inactivity.

8.    "The *Jnani* is fully aware that the true state of Being remains fixed and stationary and that all actions go around him. His nature does not change and his state is not affected in the least. He looks on everything with unconcern and remains blissful. His is the true state, the primal, natural state of Being. There is no difference between the *Jnani* and the *ajnani* in their conduct: the difference lies only in their angles of vision."    607

*Note*: The previous text speaks of the intense activity of the *Jnani*, and the first part of this text says that the Being is "fixed".

Action appears as such only in the context of sense-perceptions. In order to perceive, energy is needed, more so if it is followed by thinking and physical acting. Where does this energy come from? Certainly not from outside the perceiver, thinker and actor, but from inside himself, from his very be-ing. Thus the Being is the source of all energy, the fullness of energy, nay, Energy itself. Therefore the *Jnani* who is ever aware of this Being, ever merged in the Being, is himself this massive Energy. The Being is said to be inactive, because it is ever changeless, though ever full. And it is because it is ever full as the Eternal Consciousness-Energy that the last text compares it to the intensely spinning top which appears to be standing stark still. Thus the *Jnani* is inactive as the changeless Being, and active as the Infinite Energy itself. The paradox is thus resolved. The activity of sense-perceptions in the *Jnani* remains as an appearance in him, as we have already studied.

Therefore the *Jnani* is literally Brahman in a physical

body, the "mind is only surmised in a *Jnani*" (text above). He enjoys the senses without being imprisoned by them — his being only "*vasanas* for enjoyment". His life is pure light to his disciples, an inspiring ideal to the ordinary admirers, a focus of wisdom and peace to the wisdom and peace seekers, and a silent blessing to the whole world. Of Him Sri Krishna spoke the lines:

> "Flee unto Him for shelter with all thy being, O Bharata. By His Grace thou shalt obtain supreme peace, the everlasting home."

ending with:

> "Thus hath wisdom, more secret than secrecy itself, been declared unto thee by Me. Having reflected on it fully, then act thou as thou listeth."
>
> (*Bhagavad Gita*, XVIII, 62-63)

APPENDIX

# KEVALA KUMBHAKA

*Kevala* means alone and *kumbhaka* retention of breath, that is, without inhaling and exhaling, which highly-trained yogis can maintain for a long time at will. Some of these can remain for weeks and months — some say even years — in *kumbhaka* with the mind in coma (*laya*) without dying, because though the breath is presumed to have entered the *sushumna* and has been completely suspended, a filament of breathing still persists to sustain the life in the body. But this is not as astounding an achievement as it appears to be, nor is it indicative of advanced spirituality; for it is a purely mechanical feat of which any eligible person who undergoes the training is capable. In whatever *guna* the mind happens to be at the moment, the breath remains throughout stuck to the *nadi* which belongs to that *guna* inside the *sushumna*; for there is no *sadhana* to lift it up to a higher *guna* or to the *guna*-less state. Thus long-drawn-out *kevala kumbhaka* without *sadhana* is utterly useless except as a demonstration in endurance. *Sadhana* purifies the mind which induces alike purity in the breath.

When *kevala kumbhaka* is associated with *sadhana* it is of short durations and is often called *Yoga-samadhi*, sometimes even *nirvikalpa-samadhi*, which fundamentally differs from its namesake of the *Jnana marga* in which the mind merges completely in Brahman, the Absolute Consciousness. In this as in the previously-mentioned *kumbhaka*, the breath is caught by its own *guna* in the *sushumna* and the mind is also comatose, but the object is not demonstrative, for the public eye, but genuinely *mukti*. Theoretically *kevala kumbhaka* is immensely potent in transcending the *gunas* — *tamas, rajas* and *sattva* — in the *sushumna*, as represented by the three outer *nadis*, namely *sushumna, vajrini* and *chitrini* respectively, to the innermost *nadi*, the *Brahma nadi*, which, being *guna*-less, is blissful, hence its other name *amrita-nadi* (nectareous). But this is not, strictly speaking, a *nadi* but the pure consciousness, the Supreme Self Itself. Hence when this is attained the mind is said to have become the cosmic mind and the breath the cosmic breath.

The advantage of this method, which is widely used in the *Laya* yoga, over the other *pranayama* methods, especially the *kundalini*, is supposed to lie in its simplicity and quick results; for here the tedious labour of rousing *kundalini*, the consciousness-force which lies coiled at the root of the spine, through both the *kevala* as well as the *sahita*, or ordinary, *kumbhaka* and making it move from *chakra* to *chakra* up to the *sahasrara* is obviated, though the risk of acquiring *siddhis* and the consequent falling off the path is considerably greater. But actually this is far more tedious, dangerous and of far lesser potential success than the other systems. Gaudapada and Shankara condemn *laya* on the ground that its alleged bliss is nothing but the lethargic oblivion of the misery of the active mind obtainable in *sushupti*, which thus detracts from the progress resulting from an awakened *sadhana*. Its *samadhi* is likewise a misnomer. They aver that *laya samadhi* is as harmful as desires:

> "The mind distracted by desires and enjoyment as also the mind enjoying the pleasure of oblivion (*laya*) should be brought under discipline by the pursuit of the proper means. For *laya* is as harmful as desires."
> (*Gaudapada Karika*, III, 42, with Shankara's commentary)

By the proper means Gaudapada implies the *Jnana marga* which is the safest, quickest, and the most rational of all *sadhanas*.

When the Supreme Consciousness is experienced in *jnana* through dispassion (*vairagya*) and the usual psychical practices, namely, *vichara* and *dhyana*, perennial *kumbhaka* is spontaneously achieved without deliberate attempts for it, which is the reason why the *Jnani's* breath is said to have united with the cosmic breath. The *Jnani*, being always in mental stillness, is ever in *kumbhaka*, but what may be rightly called invisible *kumbhaka*, for the breath in it appears to be as normal as that of the *ajnani*.

# GLOSSARY

The meanings of the Sanskrit words given hereunder are not necessarily technical, but commonly accepted in the contexts employed in this work.

*Abhyasi* — One practising spiritual discipline
*Adhikari* — The qualified seeker of Truth.
*Ajnana* — Ignorance of the Self.
*Amrita* — Nectar.
*Antahkarana* — See p. 178.
*Anugraha* — Grace.
*Atman* — Self, Supreme Being, ultimate Reality, Brahman.
*Avidya* — The primal nescience.
*Bhakti* — Spiritual devotion.
*Brahman* — The vast, the Infinite, the absolute Reality (Pure Consciousness in nature).
*Chaitanya* — See *Chit*.
*Chakras* — Centres of forces in the body.
*Chit* — Pure Consciousness, the nature of the Self, of Brahman.
*Dharana* — Concentration, focusing of attention.
*Dhyana* — Meditation.
*Gunas* — The three sets of qualities constituents of the manifestation — *tamas, rajas* and *sattva*.
*Ishwara* — God the creator.
*Jada* — Inert, insentient.
*Jagrat* — The waking state.
*Japa* — Repetition of a sacred word, or words.

*Jiva* — The individual, or embodied Self.

*Jivanmukta* — The Liberated one still living in a body.

*Jnana* — Knowledge of the Self.

*Jnani* — Knower of the Self.

*Karma* — See p. 27 for definition.

*Kevala Nirvikalpa* — Temporary *nirvikalpa*; *Kevala* means alone, i.e., *samadhi* alone without the presence of the world.

*Koshas* — Various sheaths, including the physical body, which wrap up the Self as *Jiva*.

*Laya* — A state of unconsciousness resembling dreamless sleep.

*Mantra* — Incantation.

*Marga* — Path.

*Maya* — Illusion.

*Mouna* — Silence, vow of silence.

*Mouni* — One who is under *mouna*.

*Mukta* — One who is Liberated.

*Mukti* — Final Liberation.

*Nadi* — Channel, nerve, along which spiritual force flows.

*Nirvikalpa* — *Samadhi* completely free from thoughts (of the world).

*Pralaya* — World dissolution

*Pranayama* — Breath control.

*Prarabdha* — Destiny (*Karma*) which is running its course in the present time.

*Rajas* — The qualities of activity (excitement, wrong actions, etc.). See *Gunas*.

*Sadhaka* — Who practises spiritual discipline.

*Sadhana* — Spiritual discipline.

*Sahaja samadhi* — Permanent awareness of the Self, even when the world is present.

*Samadhi* — The state of being aware of the Self, or Being.

*Sankalpas* — Desires, preoccupations of the mind.

*Sannyasa* — Renunciation (of the world).

*Sat* — Pure Existence.

*Sattva* — The qualities of harmony, purity (right thinking, right acting, etc.). See *Gunas*.

*Savikalpa* — *Samadhi* which retains a certain amount of thinking.

*Shakti* — Divine Power.

*Shastras* — Hindu Scriptures.

*Siddha* — Who has psychic powers.

*Siddhis* — Psychic powers.

*Sphurana* — See p. 142.

*Srutis* — Upanishads.

*Sushumna* — The main force channel or *nadi* which runs along the spinal column.

*Sushupti* — The state of dreamless sleep.

*Svapna* — The state of dreamful sleep.

*Tamas* — The qualities of darkness, of sloth, etc. See *Gunas*.

*Tapas* — Austerities, asceticism.

*Tapasvin* — The person of *tapas*, ascetic.

*Upadhis* — Adjuncts.

*Upanishads* — The philosophical portions of the Vedas, and deal solely with the means to Liberation.

*Upasana* — Worship of form.

*Vairagya* — Dispassion.

*Vairagyi* — The man of *vairagya*.

*Vasanas* — Habits of the mind, tendencies.

*Vedanta* — The philosophical system of the Upanishads.

*Vichara* — Enquiry.

*Videha* — Without a body.

*Videhamukta* — The Liberated who has discarded his body.